CW00373677

TONGUES OF ANGELS

By the same author

The treasures of Jesus
Clouds of glory
The six chaplet Rosary

ALAN ROBINSON

Tongues of Angels

ST PAULS

These stories are works of finction and there is no intentional reference to real people except for one or two well known historical characters.

Cover by Mary Lou Winters

ST PAULS
Middlegreen, Slough SL3 6BT, United Kingdom
Moyglare Road, Maynooth, Co. Kildare, Ireland

© ST PAULS 1994

ISBN 085439 471 0

Printed by Biddles Ltd, Guildford

ST PAULS is an activity of the priests and brothers of the Society of St Paul who proclaim the Gospel through the media of social communication

Contents

1

The three angry men

Three angry middle aged men met together for a drink one Saturday evening. Nick Quick was furious because his wife had refused to iron his shirts. Des Deepman was bitterly angry right through to his soul because he had been passed over for promotion at least twenty times. Ronnie Wright was angry with the local council because they wouldn't provide proper facilities for old and handicapped people.

As the three sipped their drinks Nick Quick kept muttering to himself, "I'll murder that woman one of these days." Des Deepman was thinking, "That young snipe hasn't got a clue. I'd like to shove him over the edge of a cliff." Meanwhile Ronnie Wright was trying to think of the right sort of action to take to move the local politicians.

For ten minutes the three were silent. Then Nick said, "I'm fed up."

"What's the matter?" said Des. "Is it the wife again?"

"Too bloody right," said Nick. "She's the most infuriating woman I've ever met. Do you know, she won't even iron my shirts now." He opened his jacket. "Look at this shirt I've got on. Look how crumpled it is. What's a bloke to do? I ask you!"

The other two murmured their sympathy but couldn't offer any constructive suggestions. They sipped their drinks silently for another ten minutes.

After a bit Des said mournfully, "Do you know, they've put a chap ten years younger than me in charge of the department. I've a good mind to resign. It's diabolical. He's hardly out of short trousers. And I've been slogging my guts out for twenty five years. And where has it got me? I ask you!"

The other two couldn't offer any real help but made condoling and sympathetic noises, The three men sipped their drinks silently for another ten minutes.

Then Ronnie said, "This council we've got now is an absolute shower. Do you know, they don't give a hoot that old folk can't look after themselves properly. And that handicapped people are out on the street without a proper home. It's absolutely disgraceful. I've a good mind to write to the Queen."

The other two knew that Ronnie had no intention of writing to the Queen, but they made the usual sympathetic noises.

It so happened that a stranger who looked like an angel was sitting at the next table having a quiet drink. His name was Eirenos. The angel turned round and said, "You know, I've been listening to you three grumbling. Why don't you do something constructive for a change, instead of manufacturing unhappy words all the time?"

"Who the blazes are you?" said Nick. "Why don't you mind your own frigging business!"

Eirenos smiled with such a beatific expression that the three angry men were mesmerised. The angel said, "It doesn't really matter who I am, but perhaps I could give you each a piece of advice."

The three men nodded mutely. Eirenos continued, "Nicholas, take your case, for instance."

Nick was astonished at the use of his full first name. Only his grandmother had ever called him that and she had died long since.

"If you go on the way you are doing," said the angelic stranger, "you'll end up either having a divorce or murdering your wife."

"What shall I do then?" said Nick, a note of sarcasm in his voice.

"How long is it since you told your wife you loved her? And when did you last give her a bunch of flowers?"

Nick was speechless. He had never done either since he and his wife returned from their honeymoon.

"And take you, Desmond," said Eirenos. "When did you last bring some work home? And when did you last give a cheerful good morning to everybody at work? If you go on being so bitter you'll end up as a twisted old man with no friends. And I expect the boss will sack you next week anyway."

Des was silent. But he suddenly saw himself in a new light.

Then Eirenos said to Ronnie, "You know, Ronald, your ideas are good, but it's no use being angry and not getting it out of your system. Why don't you write that letter to the Queen, or better still, become a councillor yourself, and then you can change things."

The stranger quaffed off his drink and then strolled out of the pub.

The three men were silent for another ten minutes. Then Nick said, "That's a turn up for the book."

The other two nodded sagely.

All three men took the stranger's advice. Nick Quick rapidly became one of the best dressed men in town because his wife looked after him so diligently. Des Deepman had a promotion the following year and within five years had become the boss of the firm. Ronnie Wright eventually became Mayor of the town. When he retired, one of the very caring homes for the elderly which he had campaigned for had its name changed to Deepman House.

2

Picking up
Pontius Pilate's spectacles

I had a funny dream once. During this dream I had the privilege of meeting the notorious Pontius Pilate. It happened this way. I was walking along a street in Damascus when this fat, pompous man tripped over the edge of his robe and fell flat on his face. I helped him to get to his feet and picked up his broken spectacles for him.

"By Jupiter!" he said angrily. "I'll sue the local council for not having smooth pavements."

I looked at the pavement, but it seemed smooth enough to me. However, there was a strong smell of wine on the fat man's breath, so I drew my own conclusions.

The fat man said, "Sorry, old chap. I really do get irritated over trifles nowadays."

"Are you hurt, sir?" I said.

"Goodness me, no. It would take more than that to damage an old fox like me. But let me give you a reward."

He took a purse out of his skirt pocket.

"Goodness me, no," I said hurriedly. "I've taken a vow of poverty, you know."

"That's refreshing," he said. "By the way, my name is Pontius, Pontius Pilate."

"Weren't you the one who...?" My voice trailed away with embarrassment.

"Yes, yes," he said testily. "I was the one who..." Then his voice trailed away.

I said, "By the way, my name is Brother Tristram. May I buy you a coffee?"

"Very kind of you, old boy. But I insist. My treat. You haven't taken a vow against drinking wine, have you?"

I shook my head.

"Good. I know a good bar. Just round the corner. Let's split a bottle of Galilean wine."

That sounded rather tactless to me in the circumstances, but I didn't make any comment. He led the way and I followed.

We sat down in a quiet corner. The waiter brought some white wine in a bottle of unusual shape. It resembled a naked woman. Pontius Pilate chuckled. "I'm not trying to lead you astray. They put it in bottles of this shape because drinking this little beauty is like making love. Oh, sorry, old boy, I suppose you're not allowed to do that sort of thing."

I sipped the wine and said, "I see what you mean."

His eyes twinkled. "I'll not ask you how the comparison appeals to you," he said.

"I do have a vivid imagination," I replied, "and I was young once. But tell me Herod... sorry... I mean Pontius... have you found out the truth yet?"

"How do you mean?" he said.

"Well, you know, when you made that famous comment. 'What is truth?' I think it was. Is it true that you said that?"

"Yes," he said sadly. "But I'm no nearer the answer. Each time I think I've found it, the thing runs away again. Do you know what I mean? It's as slippery as an eel."

"I'm not quite sure I'm with you," I said.

"Well, it's like this. Having made a king sized fool of myself by asking the question, I thought I'd better try to find the answer. I thought about it for five hundred years and concluded that truth must be inside a person. There's an old proverb, you know, 'To thine own self be true.'"

"It sounds sensible to me," I said, and then waited for him to continue.

11

"The trouble is, when I thought about it, I realised that truth does lie within the self, but only one little segment of the truth, not the full circle."

"I see," I said thoughtfully. "You mean the truth is bigger than the human container can grasp."

"I didn't exactly say that," he said irritably. "The mind can grasp truths outside itself. It stand to reason. Look at the table. It's square. True or false?"

"I see," I said. "Yes, I do see."

He continued: "And then I came to the conclusion that the truth must lie in the outside world, in things I can touch, or hear, or see."

"Very good," I said, "so truth has two aspects – the inner truth and the outer truth."

"It's fairly obvious you've not given the subject much thought," said Pontius Pilate. "Truth has more than two sides to it, surely. Another definition I formulated goes like this. Truth is the way things are."

"That should cover everything," I said optimistically.

"You think so?"

"Well, surely it covers the inside truth, the outside truth and the truth as God knows it. That's everything, isn't it?"

"Of course it isn't," he snapped. "Things keep changing. Nothing ever stands still. So I then decided that the truth must be an expanding concept."

I decided it would be wiser neither to agree nor to disagree. He added, "That includes the past and the future, as well as the way things are. It also covers the way things ought to be."

A gleam of light came into my mind. I almost shouted eureka, but managed to control myself. Instead I said, "And the opposite of truth is trying to prevent things being what they ought to be, or what they really are."

"You know, Brother Tristram," said Pontius Pilate, "you're a bit more intelligent than you look. May I pour you another glass of wine?"

"Thank you," I said.

We sipped our wine reflectively for a couple of minutes. Then I said, "Is that it then?"

"Not quite," he said. "The big mistake people make when they're looking for a capital T truth is that it doesn't actually exist on its own. It's not a thing in itself. It is only an attribute of other things, or events, or attitudes. The chap who defined it as a noun got it all wrong. It's really an adjective."

I felt the wine beginning to take effect. My mind was as clear as as a pool in which I could see the pebbles as big as boulders. I said confidently, "So what we're looking for is the True?"

"Do you really think so?" he said. "I'm still not so sure. The same old question keeps coming into my mind. It hammers away in every corner of my brain. 'What is truth?' it keeps saying, over and over again. 'What is truth?'"

With that he walked away and left me to finish the bottle of wine on my own. I felt a bit miffed really. Still it was a delicious wine.

I wondered afterwards whether Pontius Pilate had been condemned to ponder his famous question for eternity, as a sort of punishment.

3.

The prison mouse

I was a prison chaplain once. It was quite a chastening experience. One prisoner I ministered to was in solitary confinement. He had been condemned to death eleven years previously. Because of frequent changes of government no Secretary of Life and Death had been able to get the penalty through the Senate. It was necessary in that country for each and every death penalty to be ratified by the Senate. The only thing is the government had to be in power for twelve months before such a decree could be ratified. However, over the period in question no goverment had lasted for more than eleven months. Needless to say, Jack Spero was a very depressed man. He didn't know whether to be glad he was alive, despite the miserable conditions in which he existed, or whether he should pray for death's final release.

One day, after I had been visiting him every week for about six months he told me a very odd story. He said, "You know, Brother Tristram, I have regular conversations with a mouse."

I was sure he had flipped his lid. But after a moment's thought I concluded that it was possible he had talked to a mouse. After all, mice could live almost anywhere. What I did find difficult to swallow was the idea that the mouse might have talked to him. All this passed through my mind in an instant. I said cautiously, "It's helpful sometimes to get things off your chest. I suppose the mouse listens well."

Jack Spero smiled briefly. He said patiently, "It's a dialogue, not a monologue."

I then concluded that he must be having strange day

dreams and that he was really having conversations with his conscience which seemed to him to have taken on a living form. I said, "Do you want to tell me about it?"

"I would like a second opinion," he said. "My friend, you know who... has given me some advice. I want to know if you agree."

"I'll be happy to give you my opinion," I said.

"Very well. I'll tell you what the mouse told me."

* * *

The first time the mouse appeared I thought I was dreaming. Anyway, he is a very polite mouse. He asked me if I had finished with my dinner and if it would be O.K. if he had a share. To be truthful, my appetite isn't what it used to be, so I invited him to go ahead. When he had finished eating he cleaned his whiskers and came to sit beside me. He said, "You look depressed Mr Spero."

I said, "You might as well call me Jack. Yes. I'm very depressed. Wouldn't you be if you were living in conditions like this."

"Oh, I don't know," he said. "I do live here you know. And I'm not depressed."

"But you aren't condemned to die any day," I said.

"You wouldn't say that if you saw all the mousetraps I come across every single day. An absolute menace they are. I'll tell you what you need. You should have a special hope, just to keep you going like. I've got one. I'm always thinking about it and it takes my mind off all my mates who've been killed recently."

"What kind of hope?" I said, without much enthusiasm.

"Well, I know it sounds a bit daft, but I hope one day I'll live on a cheese farm where the farmer doesn't have a cat. Whenever I get depressed I switch on my hope and everything improves right away."

"I see," I said. "But what could I hope for. If I hope to

15

die I'll probably go to hell for what I've done. If I hope to get a pardon I would never get a job with my record, so I would starve to death. It's horrible living here, but at least I'm alive and not in hell."

"That's a tricky one," said the mouse. "Let me think. You could always hope to get married. After you've got a pardon, I mean. Then your wife could get a job."

"I couldn't really believe in that," I said. "Who would want to marry a murderer."

"Plenty of women would," he said. "There's nothing like a tickly feeling down the spine for encouraging love. I should know. I've been married fourteen times. But all my wives fell into traps."

"No. It's no use," I said. "I haven't a hope in hell of getting married, or of getting out of here."

"I know what you need," he said, a speculative look in his eye. "You need to say a prayer. Then you'll have a hope. I once lived with a vicar, you know. His prayers kept him going, I can tell you. With a wife like his he certainly needed some help."

"Suppose God isn't there," I said. "And even if he is, will he listen to a murderer?"

"I walked over an open Bible once," he said. "I remember some of the words, maybe not exactly, but it was something like, 'God loves everybody and usually lets them off if they say they're sorry.' You could try that I suppose."

After the mouse had gone I took his advice and said a prayer. The next time the mouse came for dinner I told him what I'd done. He said, "Have you got a hope now?"

I said, "I'm not sure. I asked God to forgive me but he didn't reply. I did feel just a little bit better. It's my only hope, really. I know I'm never going to get out of here except in a coffin."

"Good," he said. "Keep it up. Your hope will grow bigger every day, you'll see."

The mouse never came back. I concluded he must have been trapped.

"So that's about it, Brother Tristram. I've been praying ever since. And I think the mouse was right. I do have some hope. But is it a true hope? Or am I living in cloud cuckoo land?"

I decided not to question the veracity of Jack Spero's story about the mouse. Instead I said, "Hope is a wonderful thing. It keeps people going in the most desperate..." I, paused, wondering whether I was going to depress him again.

"I know what you mean," he said. "I've concluded that hope is a relative thing. You can hope to win a fortune or you can hope to marry a lovely girl. Those are all right in their way. But that hope which is of true value is the one which is eternal. Nobody can ever take it away from you."

I said, "You didn't really need my advice. You've already made up your mind."

"I hope so," he said. "But I can tell from your face that you agree with the mouse. It was really that little fellow who convinced me. I thought, 'Goodness me, if a mouse can have hope, surely I can.'"

I didn't see Jack Spero again. I was called back urgently to my monastery a week after that last conversation with him. I did notice in the press, though, that the other day a new government was elected in that unhappy country. The new President said he was sure that his government would last for the full five year term.

I have thought about Jack Spero's experience many times and I have come to the conclusion he was right. Human hope is a worthwhile commodity at any time, but if it is related to God it is probably one of the most valuable treasures in human life – or death. A true hope will triumph over any human despair.

4

The Daily Tattler

It must be admitted that it is fascinating to talk about people, especially when they are about to be born, or about to be married or about to be buried. There was once a man who loved gossip and, indeed, he always said it was the only interest he had in life, apart from keeping body and soul together.

Tom Tattler lived in a respectable market town on the borders of Suffolk and Essex. While it wasn't possible to know every single person in the town by name, it has to be said that Tom knew most of them and also quite a lot about them. He could tell you the names of the great grand parents of at least half of the people who lived in the town.

Tom was a postman. That is how he came to know so much about other people's business. Not that he tampered with the mail, mind you, but it was if he had telepathic knowledge of the contents of most of the letters and parcels that he delivered. He was extremely irritated when a plain brown envelope addressed in a strange hand had to be put through somebody's letter box.

It was natural enough that people should tell Tom Tattler tasty bits of news. Most of what he was told was harmless enough, and anyway he abhorred telling lies. Still it was nice to walk his daily round saying to people, "Have you heard that Jim Biggar is putting up for the council?" or "Did you know that Mrs Heaton has won the pools?" The local newspaper proprietor would have been jealous of Tom Tattler if Tom had not been of so much help to the Argos. He dropped many a tip to the editor and had often been the inspiration behind some of the best front page stories. So Mr Dixon, the owner of the paper, used to say philosophically every Monday morning, "I wonder what time Tom Tattler is calling today?"

There was one family in the town that kept itself to itself and minded its own business. Tom had never ever been able to retail the smallest piece of gossip about this particular family whose name was Smithson. However, one day he was walking down the lane next to the Smithson's house and over the wall he overheard Mr and Mrs Smithson talking.

Mr Smithson was saying, "When is the baby expected then, Betsy?"

"She says March, but I can't help wondering if she's got the date right. It doesn't add up to me."

That was all that Tom heard, but everybody knew that the Smithson's daughter had been working in London for some time. There had been no news of any marriage. Therefore, she must have got pregnant out of wedlock. In that particular town at that particular time sex outside marriage was very much frowned upon, especially by the church and chapel folk.

As he went round Tom told everybody this exciting piece of news. He was very pleased with himself. At last he had found a piece of interesting gossip about the Smithson family. By nightfall everybody in the town knew that Julia Smithson was going to have a baby. Everybody also knew that Mr Smithson was going to murder the father for ravishing his daughter long before any wedding was planned. This was not surprising, everybody said, because the Smithsons were strong chapel folk. And in any case, it just showed you what happened to people who were foolhardy enough to go and work in London. It was all right to go there on a visit, but to live there – that was asking for trouble.

Nobody saw the Smithsons for about a fortnight after this news had been retailed on the bush telegraph. It was not, of course, a matter that would be of any interest to the Argos. This apparent absence had been noted by the wiseacres in the town and they all said that the Smithsons had gone to London to sort out the problem.

Then one morning when Tom Tattler was passing the Smithson's house he noticed an empty hearse parked in the drive. To do Tom justice he did not embroider this interesting piece of information himself. All he said to people was, "There was a hearse at the Smithson's this morning, had you heard?"

By nightfall two different stories were circulating. One version was that the Smithson girl had committed suicide because she couldn't face her parents. The other version said that Mr Smithson had been so upset by his daughter's pregnancy that he had had a fatal heart attack. The following day the Methodist minister knocked on the Smithson's door. He was quite concerned because they hadn't been to chapel for several weeks. However, there was nobody at home.

The next development was that Mr Smithson's boss was supposed to have said that he had given Mr Smithson one month's leave without pay, but apparently the boss and the other employees were very tight lipped about the reason for this leave of absence. Meanwhile nobody had caught sight of anybody in the Smithson family and the house was apparently empty. Certainly there were plenty of people watching for signs of life. Old Mrs Green swore she had seen a curtain twitching at the house, but nobody else corroborated this story. Some said that Mrs Greeen's eyes weren't what they used to be and, anyway, one of her eyes was always watering.

Everybody was completely mystified when an advertisement about the Smithson's house appeared in the Argos. It simply said the 35 Hawthorn Avenue was to let as a furnished property.

The editor of the Argos said that the advertisement had

been placed by a man he had never seen before, but he was almost sure the man had arrived in an empty hearse.

The stories about the Smithsons became wilder and wilder. One tale said that the whole family had been killed in a plane and that there hadn't been enough pieces left of the bodies for a normal Christian burial. The Argos editor checked this out, but he couldn't find any reports of a recent plane crash in any of the nationals. He spent hours in the library reading back numbers. Another version said that the father of the Smithson girl's baby had gone berserk and killed the whole family out of spite. The man from the Argos poured cold water on that theory, though, because he said it would have been on all the front pages. Yet another story, which Arnold Barnswick swore he'd got from a reliable source, said that the baby had been born prematurely and that the family had gone abroad to live because they couldn't face the shame of everybody knowing that the baby had been born out of wedlock.

Nobody applied to rent the Smithson house, even though the advertisement appeared for several weeks. There was a great silence on the subject around the town for some time, until a furniture van arrived and removed all the furniture from the Smithson's residence. A man driving an empty hearse was there, apparently to direct operations. The house was unsold for several months and then an incomer bought it and quickly moved in.

None of the imaginative theories put forward to explain these strange occurences was absolutely convincing. The Methodist minister confessed to being surprised that the Smithsons had not bothered to say goodbye, but he was sure they must have had a good reason. They were such a pleasant family.

The speculation gradually died down and several years passed. Other topics of interest took over, but none proved to be as interesting as the Smithson mystery.

Five years after the Smithsons had left the town so

mysteriously they quietly returned without a word of explanation to anybody. They bought another house in the same street. The daughter visited now and again and seemed to have come to no harm. The man with the empty hearse called now and again, but it became accepted that his visits did not signify that there had been a death in the family.

Mr Smithson returned to work for the firm where he had worked previously. The day that Mr Smithson dropped in to ask if he could have his old job back, the boss said to him, "Paul, do you remember when you left the town a few years back? What was it all about? You must admit I've not tried to pry into your affairs, but it was rather strange to have a letter from you with your resignation and no explanation. I'm happy for you to come back, of course, but how do I know the same thing won't happen again?"

"I suppose you do deserve an explanation," said Mr Smithson. "I had the chance of a lucrative job abroad but one of the conditions was that I shouldn't tell anybody about it. I worked for a goverment department during the war and this job was in the same line."

The boss thought this sounded like a dangerous sort of job, so he didn't pursue the matter. However, he told Mr Smithson about all the gossip that had gone on. Mr Smithson chuckled and said, "The baby wasn't my daughter's. It was my wife's sister's. The man in the empty hearse is my brother in law and he was keeping an eye on things for us. He happens to be an undertaker by trade."

Mr Smithson and his boss agreed to keep the town guessing for a while. Tom Tattler continued to retail interesting bits of information. The Smithson story started up again and apparently it is still talked about in the Green Parrot on Saturday nights.

Mr Smithson was heard to say once, "This a terrible town for gossip. I don't know why I came back. Fortunately most of the gossip is harmless, but one of these days somebody is going to be sued for slander."

It was Mrs Green who overheard this snatch of conversation. Before nightfall it was all over the town that Mr Smithson was going to sue Tom Tattler for defamation of character. Tom had a number of sleepless nights over this piece of intelligence, but it didn't cure him of gossiping. There is no cure for this particular human weakness.

5

The ghost of Domicilius

There was once a monk who couldn't pray. This is not a good state for a monk to be in. After all, he had sworn to devote his life to worship and to prayer, as well as to poverty, chastity and obedience.

Every morning and every evening for at least two hours on each occasion, he knelt at his prayer desk in the monastery chapel, but he couldn't find anything to say to God. At the same time, it seemed to Brother Ignatius that God didn't have anything to say to him. His spiritual life seemed to be a complete void.

Between these two prayer times he turned his eyes to heaven frequently while he was going about his daily work, which was to help the poor. However, each time he looked towards heaven and willed himself to say a prayer it seeemed as if his inner voice was dumb. Yet, many, many people had cause to thank Brother Ignatius for the way he had helped them in a very practical way. Sometimes he scrubbed a floor for a feeble old lady or perhaps he sat at a sick man's bedside all night, just holding his hand.

One morning, at the early hour of 3 a.m., Brother Ignatius was as usual on his knees in the chapel. He looked at the statue of the Blessed Virgin but received no inspiration from her. He gazed for ten minutes at the picture of Jesus being placed in his tomb, but still he received no inspiration. He then closed his eyes and tried to say the Lord's Prayer, but he just couldn't get any further than the first two words. When he opened his eyes he became aware that there was somebody else in the chapel.

He looked sideways and saw that there was a man sitting further along on the same pew. He didn't recognize the man, who was dressed in a red robe decorated with yellow flames. The stranger chuckled, but it was not a very nice chuckle. He said, "So you can't pray, eh?"

Brother Ignatius nodded miserably. The man asked, "So you're ready to give up your faith, are you?"

Brother Ignatius felt the shock of this question pulsing through his soul. It stabbed like a knife. But still he didn't reply.

The man said, "Let me introduce myself. I'm Antigabriel. I used to be an angel, but like you I lost my faith. It's not all that bad you know. You can become an ordinary person again if you like. Then you can do what you want and commit any so called sins that appeal to you. Which particular sin is it that attracts you? Actually, you needn't tell me, Ignatius. I know already. It's power, isn't it? You've been wanting to be Prior for years and your heart is very bitter. But if you leave the monastery, Ignatius, you can take power. You don't have to wait to be given it."

Brother Ignatius already knew that, but to have this unpalatable truth spoken out loud was not pleasant. Still he did not respond to Antigabriel's persuasive questions.

Antigabriel then said, "I'll leave you to it. I've never seen anybody with such a poverty stricken spiritual life. If you have any sense you'll take my advice."

Ignatius stayed in the chapel for a while but he couldn't put the vision of Antigabriel out of his mind. At length he sighed and left the chapel. During the day he worked away as usual. He comforted a bereaved woman as best he could. He helped a homeless man to find a hostel. He washed the body of a man dying with aides. He was tired out at the end of the day, so after a shorter spell than usual in the chapel he went to bed. From force of habit he wakened at 2.30 a.m. and made his way to the chapel.

He kneeled in a position of prayer. At last he managed

to find some words to say. He said aloud, "Lord, I can't go on. I think I must give up my vocation."

The statue of Our Lady remained impassive. The chapel was still except for – or was it his imagination – a wicked chuckle from behind the altar. He couldn't say another word. For the rest of his two hour vigil he was dumb, until, just as he was thinking of getting up to leave, he noticed a man standing by the altar. As in the case of Antigabriel he didn't recognize the man, who was tall of stature and was dressed in a white robe. There seemed to be a light shining round the man's head. Ignatius didn't say anything. When the figure began to move towards him Ignatius felt a tickly sensation on his arms and legs. He shivered. He wasn't exactly frightened, but he had an intuition he was in the presence of someone special.

The stranger stopped in front of Ignatius and smiled at him. Ignatius smiled back uncertainly. The man said, "I understand you have had a visit from my wicked brother, Antigabriel?"

Ignatius nodded. The man then said, "I'm Domicilius. What seems to be the trouble? Can I help?"

Ignatius tried not to burst into tears, but his eyes filled and one or two tears trickled down his cheek.

"Here," said Domicilius, "borrow my handkerchief."

Ignatius took the handkerchief and wiped his eyes. Domicilius said, "Why don't you tell me all about it?"

Ignatius managed to find his tongue and said, "I can't pray. I sit here for hours and I just can't pray. And I'm jealous of my superior. I think he's stupid and that I could do his job much better."

"That's not good," admitted Domicilius, "especially the bit about your superior. But hang on a minute while I make a communication."

Domicilius put his head in his hands and closed his eyes as if he were concentrating. After about two minutes he relaxed and opened his eyes. He said cheerfully, "Our

26

records tell me that you are constantly helping people. It seems that every day you give help to somebody."

"It is my job," said Ignatius. "I'm only doing my job."

"But you are doing it very well," said Domicilius. "Don't you realise that every good deed you do is a prayer. You are really very close to God. When you kneel in the chapel for hours he is listening to your heart speaking, not your mouth."

Ignatius said, "But I feel terrible because I can't communicate. Even if I could say the Lord's Prayer it would be a help."

"Do you read the Bible regularly?" asked Domicilius.

"Of course," said Ignatius.

"Then I advise you to read Matthew's Gospel. Chapter 5 verse 3."

With that Domicilius glided towards the altar and then his figure simply faded away. There was a Bible on the shelf in front of Ignatius. He opened it to the text quoted by Domicilius. He read, "Blessed are the poor in spirit, for theirs is the kingdom of heaven."

He felt as if a great weight had been lifted from his heart. Before he knew what was happening he was saying the Lord's Prayer and got through to the end of it without any difficulty.

It was then he remembered that he still had Domicilius's handkerchief in his hand. He shouted "Excuse me...". But then his voice trailed into silence as he realised that Domicilius had gone. He examined the handkerchief curiously. It was white and plain except that in one corner there was an embroidered initial D. Ignatius brought the handkerchief to the chapel every time he came, hoping to be able to return it. But Domicilius never reappeared.

Many months later Ignatius happened to be strolling near the graveyard of the monastery. For no conscious reason he went over to look at some of the inscriptions. To his surprise the first one he read was a dedication to a fifteenth century monk called Domicilius.

6

The man who
didn't commit a murder

I once met a man who went through all the stages of
committing a premeditated murder except the last one – he
didn't actually do the deed. However, after this strange
experience he truly felt that he understood why it is wrong
to commit a murder. The immorality of such an offence
may seem obvious to most people, but after listening to the
man's account I felt that I, too, understood the consequences of murder more fully. The man, whose real name I
shall conceal for obvious reasons, told me about this episode in his life while we were sitting together on a train
going from Ostend to Athens.

When I entered the compartment there was no one else
there and I was looking forward to an enjoyable read. With
this in mind I had brought an Agatha Christie with me. Just
before the train set off an elderly, bearded man opened the
door and struggled in with a heavy case which he lifted
onto the rack with quite a bit of heaving and pushing. Then
he flopped onto the seat opposite, panting loudly and wip-
ing his brow with a huge green handkerchief. He had a
heavy crop of grey fuzzy hair. His beard, which was rather
untidy, was grey, but still tinged here and there with its
original black. His face was redder than his exertions war-
ranted and I concluded that he was either a drinker or that
he had high blood pressure. Neither of us spoke for a few
minutes. Naturally, I was plunging avidly into my mystery
novel.

After a while my unsought for companion cleared his
throat and said, "I see you're a monk."

As I was wearing my habit it did not take a Hercule

Poirot to draw this conclusion. I lowered my book and said, "Yes, I am. Are you interested in religious matters?"

He nodded vigorously, but said, "I once nearly committed a murder, you know."

This was a fairly surprising thing for anybody to say and in the context it seemed like something of a non sequitur. Then I saw him glance at the cover of my book and I perceived his train of thought.

"It sounds as if you didn't actually do so," I said encouragingly, putting down my book. If there is one thing I prefer to a good novel it is an exciting autobiography, especially if it is told by the author himself. Of course, I persuaded myself that I might be able to give the man some spiritual advice, but in that assumption I was wrong. He had already had appropriate counselling from a much wiser source than myself – that is his own conscience. I say from his "conscience", because that is the only conclusion I can come to.

The man needed no encouragement. He started off as if he were as dedicated as Coleridge's Ancient Mariner and had to tell the tale to everyone he met. "My name is Raymonde Francois," he began, "and I used to live in London because I married an English woman. She was very beautiful and I still miss her terribly."

I murmured some sympathetic noises.

Hardly noticing, he continued, "The only trouble with Marina was that she loved everybody. After we had been married for three years I found out through the good offices of a friend that she was having an affair. I refused to believe this story, but I hired a private detective and he assured me, after due investigation, that the charge was true. She was meeting a man called Sir Rudolf Wisden at least once a week in his London flat. My family honour was trampled upon by this sordid affair and I felt I had to do something about it. I pondered the matter and decided that I could never kill my wife, though I felt I would be

29

fully justified in doing so. If I killed her then I wouldn't be able to make love to her myself, so it was – how do you English put it – cutting off my nose to spite my face.

"The only reasonable alternative would be to kill my wife's lover, then to face her with what I had done. In this way she would surely be cured of her amorous proclivities, I thought. I felt certain I could do the murder in such a way that there would be no proof, but I also felt that I could convince my wife that I had actually done the murder and that it was not a tale I had invented. What I mean is, she might think somebody else had committed the murder and that I was being an opportunist. It would be very easy for her to come to that conclusion, you understand, because I am normally a very kind and sympathetic person."

M. Francois made this claim with calm conviction and an entire lack of seemly modesty. He went on, "I shall not go into the nasty details of my plan. It is sufficient to say that I had everything ready to carry out my intention when something intervened to prevent me."

He paused and looked at me to judge the effect of this dramatic utterance. I tried to look suitably impressed.

He waited for several seconds before resuming his story and I wondered whether he had finished. However, he said with even more dramatic force, "I had a vision. I saw my long dead mother and she warned me against carrying out my plan."

"I suppose this was while you were asleep," I said, assuming he had had a dream.

"Not at all," he said. "It was night time, but I was wide awake. My wife was away at her sister's, or so she said, and I was alone in the house. I was drinking a glass of wine just before I went to bed. Then, quite without any premonition I was suddenly aware that my mother was standing in front of me. She looked just as I remember her, young and beautiful. She was not smiling. In fact, she

30

looked so stern and uncomprising that I felt as if I was in the nursery again.

"She spoke very softly: 'Raymonde, you must not do the wicked thing that is in your mind.'

"I plucked up courage and said, 'Mamma, this man has besmirched the honour of our family. It is my duty to kill him.'

"She said softly, 'If you do you will undoubtedly go to hell. It is to prevent that that I have come to speak to you.'

"'Mamma, I must do it. I simply must do it.'

"'No, Raymonde, you will not do it. What you plan to do is to steal a person's life. No human being has the right to do that. You are stealing another person's way to salvation.'

"I said, 'I'm sorry, Mamma, I have to do it.'

"Her reply was devastating to me. She said, 'What you are about to do is to put yourself into the place of God. There is no forgiveness on either side of the grave for deliberately doing such a thing, especially when you have had a warning. It was not easy for me to obtain permission to appear to you in this way.'

"My mother then smiled and the vision began to fade, but she said before she disappeared, 'Remember, Raymonde, you have never disobeyed me.'

"That was what happened," said M. Francois. "I can tell you that I never slept a wink all night and when morning finally arrived my hair was as grey as you see it now."

I said to him, "So you obeyed your mother?"

He said, "Yes, but the strange thing is the day I had planned to do the murder, Sir Rudolf Wisden, my wife's lover, died of a heart attack. It was as if my mother had some foreknowledge of his death. She saved me from committing an unnecessary murder, but she also saved my soul from hell. And I can tell you, dear sir, that I had a foretaste of hell the night following my dear mother's appearance."

We didn't talk much after that revelation. However, I couldn't concentrate on my Agatha Christie, so I shut my eyes and pondered the story I had just heard. My conclusion was that hell is a very real place. I, too, have been there just now and again.

7

Going overboard

There was once a young man called Alex who was left a fortune by his maternal uncle. Against the advice of his parents Alex left home and went to live in a large city where he indulged in all kinds of pleasures.

First of all he decided to eat and drink in all the best restaurants and night after night he gave huge dinner parties which usually had at least seven courses and ten different kinds of wine, not to mention the liqueurs and the brandies which always followed each meal. To be fair to Alex he did take his pleasures one at a time. For example, when he was indulging his stomach he was not at the same time pursuing beautiful women.

One morning, several months after he had become a gourmet, Alex arose from his bath, dried himself off and examined his naked body in the mirror. To his horror he saw that he was developing a paunch, that his eyes were puffy and that his cheeks were swollen. His complexion was much redder than he remembered from the last time he had looked critically at himself in the mirror. He immediately took a resolution to hold no more parties and to place himself on a strict diet.

It has to be said that Alex was not a person who did things by halves. Within three months he was like a skeleton and he was shunned by all his former friends. His parents came to visit him about this time and they were horrified at his emaciated appearance. After much cosseting by his mother Alex began to eat normally and after a few weeks was back to his old self, that is, the self he had possessed before he started to enjoy the unbridled pleasures of eating. His parents went home, satisfied that their son was on the road to health.

It was then that Alex became enthusiastic about the opposite sex. With all the money he had he was able to find lots of attractive company. In fact, he was soon at the stage of sleeping with a different girl almost every night, and sometimes with several girls at the same time. After six months of this kind of excess, a further examination of his image in the bathroom mirror convinced Alex that he was in danger of losing his health again, so he decided to live like a celibate and not to have anything more to do with girls.

It was a few weeks after that when Alex went to a religious meeting. It was the sort of meeting where the newcomers were targeted. At this particular meeting Alex was mesmerised by the speaker and he had no hesitation at all when he was asked to step forward to commit himself to that particular faith. He was as good as his word. He immediately became a very spectacular member of that religious denomination and even stood on a soap box in the local park to tell the populace all about his new found faith in God. He went to meetings every evening and to at least four meetings every Sunday. He was asked to lead a study group and did so with great enthusiasm. He even became convinced that God had chosen him as a special messenger to convert all the people in that country to his particular brand of religion. He took to wearing a cloak and an eastern head dress. He also grew a beard – and to be sure he began to look very prophetic. Mind you, there was one step he was unwilling to take. He could not bring himself to give all his money away. However, some higher power took a hand and the stock market had a crisis. One morning Alex found a single letter on his door mat. It bore some very bad news indeed. Not only had he lost all his money, but he was actually in debt to the tune of ten thousand pounds. Fortunately his parents were able to bail him out.

Alex was now in something of a quandary. He couldn't believe in a God who had allowed him to lose all his money. After sitting for hours in his favourite arm chair he decided that he would become an atheist. True to his character, Alex went overboard in this direction too, and he joined a philosophy society where the members used long words as a matter of course and poured scorn upon those unfortunate people who believed in a God who was as unseen as he was uncaring.

Alex stayed with the philosophers' club for about six months. At first he was the embodiment of enthusiasm and quoted Bertrand Russell frequently and with great gusto. At length, however, he became tired of his fellow philosophers and their pompous posturing. One Wednesday evening he went to see a film instead of going to take part in the great debate on the subject of the Reality of Tables and Chairs. He sat comfortably in the cinema seat munching chocolates and thinking nonchalantly about the pleasant reality of his surroundings.

For some time after that Alex pondered the great questions about the meaning of life. One day he found a book about Saint Francis in the local bookshop. As soon as he had read three pages he knew that he was destined to be a religious. With his usual enthusiasm he immediately took steps to further this calling. That was how I came to meet him.

Actually, his name was not Alex. I have used that pseudonym in order to spare the man's blushes. He came to our monastery one day, knocked on the door, and asked if he could join the order. The superior sent for me. I thought that was a bit unfair really, but the Abbot was convinced quite erroneously that I knew something about psychology. I was introduced to Alex and we sat down together to talk through his conviction that he should become a monk. It was three quarters of an hour before I could get a word in.

35

After very little prompting Alex told me his whole life story, including all the details I have so far related. I soon realised that we were on a wild goose chase. After about three hours I decided to give Alex a piece of advice. I nearly always give the same advice to would be postulants. I told him to come back to the monastery twelve months to the very day so that we could talk further about his vocation.

"But Brother Tristram," he objected, "I want to start today. Suppose I don't wish to join in twelve months time?"

What could I say? I let him down lightly and said it was the usual thing to wait for twelve months before deciding. I also gave him a further piece of advice. I said to him, "Why don't you try a bit of moderation? It's an old fashioned virtue and used to be called temperance. Your life is just like a game of tennis. First you dash off enthusiastically in one direction, and you dash off enthusiastically the other way. I'm surprised you haven't had a nervous breakdown."

Alex beamed at me as if he had suddenly seen the light. "Do you know," he said enthusiastically, "I believe you're right. That's what I'll do. I'll start right away. Moderation is the key word from now on."

He shook my hand until I thought it would drop off and then he shot off as if he had an appointment with the Prime Minister at least.

I marked my diary for that date a year hence. I was not surprised when Alex did not turn up. I had been hopeful, of course, that my advice would be taken seriously. But I knew my hope was a vain one when I read in the local press that Alex was standing as a candidate in the elections for the borough council. The headline read, "THE INDEPENDENT CANDIDATE IS ALL FOR THE EQUALITY OF THE SEXES." The word enthusiastic appeared at least seven times in the following article.

8

A lie for a life

There are lies, there are half lies, there are white lies, there are black lies, there are exaggerated lies, there are unintentional lies, there are neverending catalogues of lies – but there is only one truth. However, to try to live entirely by the exact truth would be a little unwise. For example, to tell your Aunt Molly precisely what you think of her hair do might persuade her to buy you a less expensive birthday present. On the other hand, untruths can sometimes do so much serious damage that it is undoubtedly a good principle to try to live in the light of the truth, if not by the absolute literal truth.

That reminds me of a man I once met who was the victim of a very damaging untruth. I heard about Robin Lobley long before I ever met him. He was well known in the locality where I lived at that time as a murderer who had never been brought to justice. Everybody knew for certain that he had killed his wife. Even the police were certain he had done the deed. However, the body of Robin's wife was nowhere to be found and the evidence rested upon the word of one man who swore he had seen Robin putting a body in the boot of his car at midnight shortly after his wife had disappeared. However, there was simply not enough evidence for a court case to be brought. The police had kept Robin in custody for questioning for as long as was legally allowed, but he wouldn't move from his story.

Essentially, Robin said that his wife had left him and gone to live abroad. Unfortunately for him she had left no forwarding address and Interpol could not trace her. The police had dug the Lobleys' garden extensively, but all they had found was a button from one of Mrs Lobley's dresses. The Inspector in charge of the case said pompously that this was "circumstantial evidence" that her body had been in the garden, but that Lobley had been sharp enough to move it, as had been testified by the man who lived opposite, one Hermann Vorst. Robin admitted that he had carried several small parcels to the car, but swore they were merely some old things belonging to his wife that he wanted rid of. There were those who claimed darkly that Lobley must have cut up the body to enable him to dispose of it more easily. At the same time Vorst would not change his story. He claimed that a huge sack had been carried to the car, not several smaller parcels.

So matters stood for about two years. Then it was that a new piece of evidence materialised. A second man came forward to support Hermann Vorst's story about Robin Lobley putting a heavy sack into the boot of his car. He had not come forward previously, he claimed, because he had gone into hospital a day or two after the night in question and had then gone to live with his daughter in a different part of the country. The situation had now completely changed. Now it was a case of the word of two men against the word of one. Robin Lobley was charged with the murder of his wife and was eventually found guilty.

At that time the death penalty for premeditated murder was still on the statute book. It was while Robin was waiting to be hung that I first met him. In the absence of the chaplain I had been asked to minister to Robin. I got to know him quite well, as a matter of fact, and we played several good games of chess together. He was a handsome man of about fifty. He had a full head of black hair and a well tanned face. His main interests were fishing and stamp collecting. I found it difficult to believe he was a murderer, but then I have met several murderers who all went to the gallows swearing their innocence – and in every case it had seemed incredible to me that any of them could have committed murder. Yet, the evidence of the prosecution in each of those cases had been overwhelming. However, Robin Lobley's case seemed to me to be different. His story was coherent and never varied. The evidence against him was slim, to say the least. Nevertheless, the jury believed the two witnesses and Robin was unable to explain the apparent discrepancy in his own story.

Twenty four hours before he was due to be executed Robin seemed to want to have a serious conversation, which was not surprising in the circumstances. We had just finished a game of chess. He looked at me earnestly and said, "Brother Tristram, you believe in God, don't you?" Naturally I said that I did. Robin continued, "As God is my witness I did not kill my wife. But it looks as if I have to meet God himself tomorrow. He knows I am innocent. What I cannot understand is why Hermann Vorst and the other man are lying. Why doesn't God step in and do something? Why should an innocent man die?"

There was little I could say except that eventually, in this life or the next the truth would come out. I said a prayer with him and he seemed to be quieter in his spirit. The next day I was present at his execution. He was pale but composed. He made no further attempt to maintain his innocence, but before he was blindfolded he looked me straight in the eye. I was absolutely certain in my own mind that an innocent man was about to be executed, but I didn't utter a word. I knew it would have been pointless.

Three weeks after the execution Mrs Lobley turned up alive and well. There was a stir in the town that day, I can tell you. There were also some red faces. It was said that Hermann Vorst and his fellow witness looked like death when they heard the news. In fact, Vorst himself died of a heart attack before he could be further questioned by the police. The other man still stuck to his story, but those who listened said he sounded much less convincing than before.

The remaining witness was brought to court to explain himself. I happened to have some other business in the court on that day so I sat in on the enquiry. The lawyers made mincemeat of the man. It turned out that he had been too far away from Robin's car to see precisely what he had been putting into the boot. He admitted that Vorst had persuaded him that he must have seen a large sack. Later extensive enquiries were made about Vorst and it turned out that he had been convicted several times for fraud and had been to prison. It also turned out that he had had a fracas with Robin Lobley over a question of parking their cars and blocking other people's right of way. It was concluded by everyone that Vorst had deliberately told a mischievous lie.

I must say that the attitudes of most people in the town made me feel sick to the pit of my stomach. Their regrets were so superficial it was unbelievable. Some people even claimed to have believed in Robin's innocence all along – and I knew that was completely untrue, because at the time nobody had a good word to say about him.

I still wonder whether I should have spoken up at the time of the execution, but my all too little store of common sense tells me it wouldn't have made any difference. However, I always carry with me a tiny nagging doubt about the matter.

It was very odd, I think, that Vorst should have died when he did. Why couldn't he have died a few weeks earlier so that justice could have been done? But who am I to question the mysterious ways of Almighty God?

9

A lusty marriage

Maria was the daughter of the best ice cream maker in Manchester. Her father was Frederico Parlatti. He had lived in Italy until he was twenty five. He had then met a young English girl in Sorrento. They immediately fell in love and Frederico agreed to live in Britain. The couple only had one daughter and naturally, as she was born and bred in Manchester, her outlook was almost entirely British. Yet, her luxuriant dark hair, her madonna face with its olive colouring and her lithe, buxom figure were unmistakably of the south. She was Italian in every inch of her body. Moreover, every man who came within range was immediately aware of her animal magnetism. It was as if she radiated the essence of Sorrento and Capri and encapsulated the spirit of the Neapolitan sun.

When she left school Maria worked in her father's ice cream parlour. Actually, Frederico had by that time diversified and he sold sweets and coffee, as well as his delicious ice cream. He was quite well to do and the family had a beautiful house in the suburbs. Not unnaturally Maria had a number of boy friends, but she kept them at a distance. She had a very cool head and had decided to marry only when she met the right man. Her ideal lover, she thought, would be ten years older than herself, he would be a business man and he would be a good Catholic. She kept her bodily charms strictly to herself and, although all her boy friends were enraptured by her, she never allowed any of them to have more than a kiss, though it must be admitted that each kiss was as luscious as a strawberry. What Maria did not know was that there were at least ten young men who dreamed about her every night. Their dreams were so passionate that they usually woke up soaked in perspiration.

One hot summer day, which it must be admitted was not the sort of weather Manchester people were used to, Maria was sunbathing in her parents' garden. She wished they had a swimming pool, but her father argued that it wasn't worth the investment considering the number of days they would be able to swim in it. On this particular day Maria was aware that she was being watched. She was amused by this, but she had no idea of the power that lay hidden in her well proportioned limbs. It was the man who lived opposite who was watching her and, moreover, he was using binoculars. He was forty three years old and unmarried, though he was experienced sexually and had had many affairs. However, all his past loves were forgotten as he gazed lustfully at Maria's sun tanned body. He made up his mind that he was going to have her whatever the cost. The thought of taking Maria into his arms possessed him like a devil.

Maria was intrigued by the interest of the man who lived opposite. She made discreet enquiries and found that he was called Kenneth Brannagan. Moreover, he exactly matched her criteria for a marriage partner, except perhaps he was just a little older than her ideal. She made up her mind to make Kenneth's acquaintance. To the man's surprise he saw Maria walking her father's dog one evening and before she crossed the road to go home she lingered for quite a significant time opposite his house. Kenneth immediately began to work in his garden every evening about the same time. Maria continued her evening walks. It was not long before they were friends. Within a year they had become engaged. Within two years they were married. That was when Kenneth's troubles began.

During their courtship he had been very careful not to show his secret lust too openly. When they reached the marriage bed, of course, his passions were released. Maria was very inexperienced, but she took to love making easily and soon began to match her husband's passion. Indeed, she became much more passionate than he had bargained for. She insisted that that they retired to bed each evening about nine o'clock and every evening nature permitted they made passionate love for two hours at least. Kenneth soon began to look a shadow of his former self.

Nevertheless, he was still filled with lust for Maria and all day and every day he thought about nothing else but the love making session they were to have that evening. His work began to suffer and he missed a promotion. Maria was oblivious to her husband's difficulties. He was reasonably attentive and he was attractive enough for her to be proud to introduce him to all her friends. Her own thoughts of love making were confined to the bedroom. The rest of the time she thought of other things. Maria was happy, though just occasionally she felt there was some element missing from her life, but she couldn't just pin down what it was. At first she thought it was a desire to have a child, but dismissed the thought immediately as a figment of her imagination. She felt that children would arrive in God's good time. Her parents, though, were surprised when no grandchild had appeared after three years of marriage.

It was about this time that Kenneth came to ask my advice. I was helping out in the Parish of Our Lady of Lourdes at the time. When I opened the presbytery door and found Kenneth on the doorstep, I did recognise him, but I couldn't put a name to the face. I showed him into the study. He introduced himself and asked if he could talk to me privately. I indicated that private and confidential conversations were a necessary function for a priest. Immediately he plunged into the story of his marriage and within ten minutes I was possessed of all the main facts as I have already outlined them. I ought to say at this point that I have altered the story and the characters sufficiently to be

43

certain that the main participants could not be identified. Kenneth's wife, for example, was not of Italian origin at all, though certainly her parents came from warmer climes than Britain.

When Kenneth had finished I said. "So what do you want me to say?"

"I was hoping you would tell me what to do, Brother Tristram."

"I'm a celibate," I said. "What do I know about marriage?"

Actually, this was a gambit to gain his confidence. Like most priests I have received a lot of training in the area of marital problems. He said, as I knew he would, "But you can give me an objective view. How can I escape from this devil that burns inside me?"

"It's usually called lust," I said. "If it gets out of control its effects can be devastating."

"I know that," he said irritably. "I know all about the effects. But I can't very well refuse to go to bed with my wife, can I?"

"Of course not," I said. "It's your duty to give her physical love, just as it is her duty to satisfy your physical needs. Usually the problem is one of alleged frigidity by one of the partners."

He laughed a short, bitter laugh. "I can assure you that is not the case with us."

"Children might help," I said, fishing a little.

"We've tried," he said. "We've tried until I'm exhausted."

"Is your wife exhausted?" I asked.

"No. She seems to have all the energy in the world. She goes on and on but I feel I'm going to snap soon. Maybe I haven't got the stamina."

"Nonsense," I said. "Most men have the stamina if they're in good health. There's nothing wrong with...?"

"I'm in good health," he insisted.

"Then there's only one cure for your problem," I said. He looked at me hopefully.

"You aren't going to believe me."

"I'll try anything," he said. "Is it fasting or something like that?"

I laughed. "I'm sorry," I said quickly. "It isn't anything at all. It's just that you made it sound as if fasting was the cure for all ills."

"What is it then?" he said. "What's the cure?"

"It's so simple you'll think I'm potty," I said. "What you have done is separate lust from love. Your body, soul and mind are filled with physical desire. Why don't you try giving your wife a little genuine affection and love."

His eyes opened with surprise. He appeared to be struck dumb. I waited until he had fully taken in what I had said. Then I added, "That's my advice. Take it or leave it."

He now looked very crestfallen. I said hastily, "The outsider can often see the cause of a problem when the people concerned can't, because they are too close to it."

"I'll think about it," he said soberly.

It was a great pleasure about twelve months later to baptise the first child of Maria and Kenneth Brannagan. They named the boy Frederick Tristram. I must say I was extremely flattered.

10

Trial by angel

There was once an angel who was, generally speaking, of a very good character. The only thing is there was just a streak of loving mischief in the angel's heart and he did like a joke. His name was Emeth. One day he was talking to his colleague, another angel called Shafat. The latter claimed he was guarding a young woman who was as pure as the driven snow in every way.

Emeth said, "Come off it, Shafat. We all know human beings are imperfect. Even we have our faults. I really don't believe she can be as perfect as all that."

"I can assure you that she is," said Shafat huffily. "I've been guardian angel for a lot of people in my time, but this girl is special. I'm surprised she's not one of us."

"If she's as perfect as you make out," said Emeth, "perhaps you wouldn't mind if we tested her a little."

"Oh, I don't know," said Shafat. "I'm aware we're allowed to do that, but it does seem a shame to manipulate such a nice girl."

"I'll tell you what I'll do," said Emeth. "If you let me try one or two tests on her I'll do your next guardianship for you."

"If you square it with the Boss," said Shafat.

"Of course. And I'll confess the true reason."

"I should jolly well think so," said Shafat indignantly.

And so it was arranged. Emeth was given a free hand.

Naturally he had to study his subject first. He went to the office and borrowed the girl's file. He discovered that Gwendoline Morgan, as she was called, was twenty three years old. She lived in Brecon in Wales and was strong chapel. Her father was the local draper. She was the oldest of four children and she worked in her father's shop. After examining the file carefully Emeth went to Gwendoline's house to have a look at her. She was not a beauty, but she had her own quiet charm. She was a bit like a summer rose tucked away behind a hawthorn bush where few people could see her.

Emeth went back to Shafat as protocol demanded and told him what he had in mind. "I'd like to give the girl three tests," he said. "Firstly, I want to see if she can be persuaded to tell a lie. Secondly, I wish to see if she will break a promise. And thirdly, it would be interesting to know if a man can seduce her."

"That last one's a bit below the belt," objected Shafat. "She's a very innocent girl."

"I won't let it actually happen," said Emeth. "It will all be in her mind."

"Very well," said Shafat, "and suppose she passes all three tests?"

"We shall make sure she gets her heart's desire," said Emeth.

Shafat smiled mysteriously. "Very well, my friend. I only hope you can deliver the goods when the time comes."

Emeth arranged several situations in which it would have been convenient for Gwendoline to tell a lie. Just to give one example, he made her bump into a valuable vase which had stood for many years on a pedestal in the shop. When her father came and saw what had happened he assumed a customer had knocked over the vase and then fled without owning up. "Did you recognize who it was?" he said to his daughter.

Gwendoline could very easily have said that somebody else had knocked over the vase, but she looked her father straight in the eye and said, "I'm sorry, father, I knocked the vase over."

Her father was furious and gave her a good telling off.

Emeth tried other stratagems to try to persuade Gwendoline to lie, but all his efforts failed, so he went on to try the next test.

Angels are very good at organising situations. It is an essential part of the job. In this case Emeth arranged a double booking in Gwendoline's engagements. On the one hand, she promised faithfully that she would take her niece to the cinema on a particular Saturday afternoon. Emeth then created a blank in her mind so that she then arranged with a girl friend to meet two men friends, the plan being that they would go to the local rugby match. This was an important fixture and Gwendoline was mad on rugby.

On the afternoon in question Gwendoline was just giving a final pat to her hair in front of the mirror when the door bell rang and her niece appeared. At once the blank in Gwendoline's mind was removed and her memory returned. In an instant she decided to forego the rugby match and didn't even mention it to her niece. However, as they went out she whispered to her mother, "When Jenny calls tell her I've gone to the pictures with Mary. I'll see her tonight and explain."

All through the film Gwendoline wondered wistfully how the local heroes were performing on the rugby field, but not one word of regret did she express.

Emeth was pleased his stratagem had failed. He was beginning to like and respect this Welsh girl. However, he knew the next test would be a hard one, because he had arranged for the captain of the local rugby team to fall in love with Gwendoline. This particular man was desired by all the local girls and quite a few of them had surrendered their virginity to him in the back of his large motor car.

When Gareth Jones started paying Gwendoline serious attention she was at first disbelieving and thought he was playing some kind of game with her. However, Gareth persisted and finally persuaded her to go out with him. He was a very physical person, though he also had perfect manners. It was usually the girls who wanted to be seduced, not Gareth who wanted to do the seducing. He was such a pleasant fellow that he never liked to disappoint a girl. However, he was a bit put out when Gwendoline gave him no encouragement. He took this as a personal challenge and made up his mind that he was going to have her.

He sent her flowers and boxes of chocolates. When he was playing rugby he pinned onto his shirt a piece of hair ribbon he had begged from her. This went on for several weeks. Gwendoline's mother began to get worried and had a serious talk with her. Despite this, Gwendoline was very tempted. She was a normal healthy girl and Gareth was everything a girl could desire. However, she had several sleepless nights over the man and then made up her mind to give him the cold shoulder. She did things very tactfully, of course. She indicated that she wished to settle down and start a family. Gareth turned pale and made his excuses. His attentions suddenly ceased and whenever he saw Gwendoline he passed by on the other side of the street.

Emeth reported back to his colleague, Shafat, who expressed little surprise. "I knew you would fail," he said.

"That's not fair," said Emeth. "I wanted the girl to show her true colours."

"And now she has done so, what are you going to do about it?" said Shafat pointedly.

"I shall keep my word," said Emeth. "Gwendoline shall have her heart's desire. I assume you know her well enough to be able to tell me what that might be."

"I certainly do," said Shafat. "Above all else she wishes to see God."

Emeth was aghast. "You know I can't grant her that. Only the Boss himself can do something like that."

"Well," smiled Shafat innocently, "you know what you'll have to do."

Emeth looked very serious. "I know," he said. "I must pray constantly until it happens."

"Don't worry, I'll pray with you, old friend."

"Do you think we shall have to pray for a long time?" said Emeth.

"I shouldn't think so. Gwendoline already knows the Boss as well as we do. I guess it would have happened soon anyway."

11

The art of good manners

I used to live in a country where most of the people believed they had developed good manners to a fine art. I went to Cartesia as a missionary. I spent three years there and so I had good opportunities to observe the behaviour of various groups of people. I suppose it could be said that the Cartesians were divided into three classes. At the top of the pyramid were the nobility, people who could recall their ancient lineage and who were proud of their traditions. Then there were the merchants who were rich and tried unsuccessfully to become part of the nobility. Finally, there were those people who were skilled in various crafts and who produced most of the wealth of the country. The crafters, as they were called, were quite well off. Indeed, there was no real poverty in Cartesia.

The three classes of people met freely in churches, restaurants and other public places, but each class had its own exclusive private clubs and societies. I was once in a restaurant having lunch when I accidentally overheard a conversation between a noble woman and a foreigner. It was evident that the noblewoman was attempting to explain some of the country's customs. At one point she said, "Now look at those two people over there. I'm sure they are very nice people, but they have not been taught good manners. Look at the way the woman is holding her fork and look at the man's elbows. He has them in the wrong position altogether. It's easy to tell who is one of us and who is not."

The foreigner said, "But surely there is more to good manners than that."

"Of course," said the woman. "I was only giving you an example. Good manners enable civilised people to live comfortably together. They know exactly what to do and how to do it. Everybody expects a certain standard of behaviour."

I must say I felt like interrupting at that point with a comment of my own, but I felt it would have been very ill mannered of me to interrupt; and certainly, the noble woman would have found such an interruption extremely uncivilised. However, the foreigner seemed to be thinking on the same lines as myself, because he said, "I always thought good manners were about consideration for other people."

"That's absolutely right," said the noble woman, "but people who are not of our class don't understand that. That's why we make each other uncomfortable."

The foreigner made no other comment, but I could see from the expression on his face that he had concluded that his companion did not understand the full import of his remark.

Shortly afterwards I was invited to a merchant's house for dinner. There were seven people at the meal altogether. Apart from myself there were three solid looking merchants and their wives. I must say they made me very welcome and our hosts looked after my every need. Part way through the meal I asked a leading question about the three classes in Cartesian society.

One of the men said tartly, "The nobility think they know it all. To try to enter one of their circles is almost impossible. It's not as if we're the poor relations. They're the ones who are poor – well certainly not as rich as us anyway. And their manners are deplorable. They'll do business with you, then cut you dead in the street five minutes later. Now take the merchants as a group. They are full of concern for other people and they know how to make people feel welcome."

"That's true," I said. "I certainly feel very welcome

here. But what about the crafters? Would you invite one to dinner?"

There was an embarrassed silence. Then the merchant who had invited me said apologetically, "I haven't anything against them, of course, but they wouldn't feel comfortable. They don't understand our code of conduct. Mind you, it is possible for a bright young crafter to become a merchant, but he has to learn to conform to our standards of good manners."

"Could you give me an example of what you mean?" I asked curiously.

"I could give you dozens of examples," he said. "Take the way we eat. It is customary to tilt the plate away from you, not towards you. We use only forks and not knives for many dishes. You have to know when it is polite to use a knife."

"But surely," I said, remembering my previous experience in the restaurant, "good manners are about consideration for others."

"That's exactly what I'm getting at," he said. Everybody else nodded in agreement. He then continued, "If they don't know the proper code of conduct they won't know how to be considerate."

I decided discretion was the better part of good manners and I said nothing further.

On another occasion I sat beside an elderly man in the park. I guessed he was a retired crafter. Neither a noble nor a merchant would sit on a bench in a public park. Such behaviour would be considered unbecoming. After a few remarks about the weather and the local basketball team I said, "I wonder if you can help me, please? I'm trying to find out more about the manners and customs of your people."

"What would you like to know?" the man said courteously.

"How would you define good manners?" I said.

"You know I'm a crafter?" was his first reaction.

"I didn't know for certain," I said diplomatically.

"Well I am," he said, "and we have our standards. We're a very proud group of people. Now the nobles and the merchants, they have no idea what true good manners are about. They like to think they are better than us, but I've thought about it and I've concluded they are so hidebound by traditions that they can't see themselves the way others see them."

"Isn't that true of the crafters?" I said innocently.

"People at the bottom of the pile know more about true values than people at the top," he said. "After all, we don't have silver spoons in our mouths when we're born, do we?"

I nodded sympathetically. He continued, "If a noble or a merchant came to my house neither would have any idea about the correct way to behave. Our children are taught good manners when they are in the cradle, so it comes naturally. They know what to say in certain circumstances. They know when to send flowers or when to write a thank you note. It's all in the way you bring them up."

"So what is the heart of good manners?" I asked.

"Consideration for other people," he said immediately.

I was left wondering precisely what he meant. He seemed in a way to be just as confined to his class as the merchants and the nobles. All agreed that consideration for others was an important ingredient of good manners, but their particular views seemed to me to be relative to their own group.

I pondered this question for a long time and eventually I concluded that the heart of good manners lies in being able to put oneself in the place of the other person whoever that person is – and then to show concern and consideration. In other words, understanding and imagination are required before true consideration can be shown. It is certainly the depth of bad manners to allow a person to feel embarrassed because of differences in superficial customs.

12

The merciless judge

Judge Miller was merciless in his judgements, especially when it came to sentencing convicted prostitutes. Invariably he gave girls or boys who were on the game the most severe sentence he could possibly award.

I was once in Judge Miller's court when he sentenced a girl I knew. This particular girl was very beautiful and she had drifted into prostitution because of the need to buy food and clothing for her son. She was a single mother and had been put into the family way by a married man who had then abandoned her. Her parents didn't want to know either.

Rebecca was smallish, with dark hair cut very short so that she looked like a boy. Her features were fine enough for a madonna. I came across her one day in the course of my ministry in a large city. I chatted to her and discovered that she came from a Christian family. I visited her regularly at her small flat and became quite attached to Vincent, her little boy. One or two of the neighbours apparently gossiped about my visits, but I took no notice.

I did give Rebecca some money to see to the boy's needs from time to time, but the coffers of my house were not bottomless, and she insisted that she still had to entertain clients, as she called them. On these occasions she left Vincent with a neighbour.

When she was arrested for prostitution, she gave my name to her legal adviser and I agreed to appear on her behalf. My main function was to demonstrate that Rebecca had been forced onto the game by unfortunate circumstances. I believe in all modesty that I argued a good case on her behalf. The solicitor said afterwards that my appeal would have moved Adolf Hitler to tears. However, Judge Miller was unmoved.

I can see the judge now. There he sat with his supercilious smile under his ridiculous wig. His mouth had a cruel twist to it and his eyes were hard and piercing as diamonds. After the jury had found Rebecca guilty he gave a little speech about the stupidity and wickedness of women who sold their bodies for money. Then he said harshly, "The maximum sentence I can give you under this jurisdiction is five years. If I could give a longer sentence I would. Your child meanwhile will be handed over to the local authority and I pray that he will receive a good Christian upbringing."

The hypocrisy of these words made me extremely angry, but there was nothing I could do. This particular judge was notorious for putting people into gaol for contempt of court, so I controlled my natural reaction, which would have been to stand up and shout, "Have you never read the story about Jesus and the woman caught in adultery?"

I made sure that Vincent did go into a good home and I visited both him and his mother regularly, acting as a link between them.

There was a strange sequel to this story which proves, at least to me, that God is not mocked. I happened to be walking along a main street in the red light district of the same city. A car pulled up beside me and a middle aged man asked me the way to Corney Street. I regretted that I was unable to help. I thought the man's face was familiar, but I couldn't place him. However, I observed that he drove his opulent car further along the street and stopped to ask somebody else the way. Before the man had had time to ask his question properly a policeman shot out of a doorway and arrested the man. By that time I had reached the place where the car had stopped. I heard the man in the car say, "But I was just asking for directions, officer."

The policeman said tartly, "You can tell that to the magistrates. They might believe you, I'm sure."

The policeman's tone of voice indicated that there wasn't the slightest chance of even the most lenient of magistrates believing the man's story. It was then that the man in the car saw me. He shouted, "Officer, ask that monk there. I stopped him a moment ago to ask the same question."

The constable said, "I don't care if you asked the Archangel Gabriel, sir. You are under arrest."

However, the policeman did turn to me to say, "Is this true, sir?"

It was then that I recognised the man in the car as Judge Miller. I have had many temptations in my life but never have I had one so great as I had that day. I could feel the words forming on my tongue: I have never seen this man...

However, I knew deep down that I had to tell the truth so I said, "This man stopped further back down the road and asked me the way to Corney Street."

"It's a dodge that's been tried before," said the policeman sternly. "You are really a monk, are you sir?"

I said, "I'm afraid so, officer. You can contact me at this address."

I gave him a card on which was the name and address of our house.

"Very well, sir, but the arrest still stands. He may well have asked you the way, but he certainly accosted our police woman here, and I have to report back to my superior officer."

The police woman concerned was dressed in hot pants and fish net tights. She was certainly a very attractive lady.

The policeman continued, "We may need to contact you again, sir. May I keep this card?"

I said, "Of course."

The policeman then said to the man in the car, "You'll have to come with us to the police station, sir."

The judge shouted, "You nitwit, I'm a circuit judge.

You won't get away with this, I can assure you. I shall have words to say to your superintendent."

The policeman's mouth went very tight. He said, "You must do what you think best, sir. I'm only doing my duty. All the same, if you wouldn't mind coming along to the station, sir."

It was inevitable, I suppose, that there would be a court case. Once it was known that a judge had been questioned about accosting a "prostitute" there would have been a public outcry if the case had been dropped. I was called as a witness, of course. It was naturally the defence lawyer who was depending upon my testimony. The crunch came when he asked me, "Brother Tristram, in your opinion was Mr Miller genuinely asking for geographical directions?"

The prosecuting lawyer protested loudly at the way the question was put, but the judge told me to answer truthfully, I said, "I believe that was the case."

There was no doubt that my answer to that question allowed Judge Miller to leave that court without a stain on his character.

Several days later I had a caller at our house. It turned out to be Judge Miller. He was shown into the guests' parlour and there we had a very private chat. He said he had come to thank me because he knew that without me the prosecution would have crucified him. I said, "Our Lord was crucified."

He apologized immediately. "I'm sorry Brother Tristram, I didn't mean to be blasphemous."

I said, "I wasn't thinking about that. I was thinking about why our Lord allowed himself to be crucified."

He was silent. After a long pause he said, "You know, Brother Tristram, I'm sure I've seen you before somewhere."

"You have," I said. "I appeared in your court once to make a speech in support of a young girl."

"Never," he said. "I would certainly have remembered."

"I was wearing civvies," I said. "The girl's name was Rebecca. She was up for prostitution. I tried to explain that she was forced into that position by unfortunate circumstances."

To do the judge justice his face turned fiery red. I went on, "Jesus also said, 'Blessed are the merciful for they shall receive mercy.'"

He put his head into his hands and began to weep. After a while he said, "I swear I'll...".

I interrupted quickly. "Don't swear. The good book tells us not to swear in that sense. I know what is in your mind. That is sufficient."

13

The sun worshipper

I once met a man who claimed to worship the sun. It was on the question of his sun worship that I got myself into a heated argument with another acquaintance who abhorred all attempts to portray God.

It so happened that Fr O'Flynn and I were both invited to a party at the sun worshipper's house, though we didn't know he was a sun worshipper before we went. The party was to celebrate the opening of a new putting green in the small town where I was working at the time. Fr O'Flynn and I were both on the committee which had planned the putting green and Mr Smithson, the sun worshipper, happened to be the chairman of the same committee.

The party was the sort where you tried to eat sausage rolls from a cardboard plate while at the same time holding a glass of wine. I have to admit that I have become an expert in performing feasts of gastronomy while in this seemingly difficult position.

I had just finished eating when Fr O'Flynn and Mr Smithson descended upon me together to impart the information that they were going to look at Mr Smithson's private chapel which was upstairs. Although I thought this might be rather a boring experience I accepted the invitation so as not to offend our host.

As we were going upstairs Fr O'Flynn said, "Which denomination do you belong to, Mr Smithson?"

Mr Smithson replied, "I am the founder of a new denomination."

That aroused my interest immediately and I decided that

the experience might be less boring than I had anticipated. In that conclusion I was correct. It turned out to be a riveting experience.

When we entered the chapel I saw that there was an altar at one end of what I supposed had originally been a large bedroom. Above the altar was a metal disc with rays spreading outwards. Even a child would have said that this was an image of the sun. Across the front of the altar frontal was another picture of a sun with the name Akhenaton embroidered across it. There wasn't much else in the room apart from a semi-circle of chairs. Mr Smithson bowed to the altar and then said, "What do you think of my chapel then?"

I said, "What do you do when you meet?"

Mr Smithson said cheerfully, "We contemplate the image of the sun. Then we share our thoughts. That's about it really."

Fr O'Flynn was ominously silent.

It was obviously up to me to keep up the conversation so I said, "Don't you sing hymns or have a sermon?"

"No. We're a bit like the Quakers really. We wait for the Spirit of the Sun to inspire us."

"But you do believe in God?" I said.

"Of course. The sun disc is a symbol of the one God. You've heard of Akhenaton, of course?"

"Perhaps you could remind me...?" I said.

"Well, he was an Egyptian Pharaoh who did away with all the traditional gods and instituted the first monotheistic religion. He believed the sun disc was a true symbol of the nature of God. You do see, don't you? The sun brings light and life just as God does."

At this point Fr O'Flynn stalked out of the chapel and out of the house without a word of explanation.

I said, "But you don't believe God is the sun?"

"Yes and no," said Mr Smithson. "I believe God is everywhere so he must be in the sun. But of course he is bigger than all creation, isn't he?"

I certainly couldn't disagree with the last part of his creed, but I made no comment on the first part. I somehow thought it wasn't quite orthodox. I asked a few more questions and then made my excuses. I was anxious to find Fr O'Flynn to see what he thought.

When I reached the presbytery I found my colleague sipping a glass of Irish whisky. Moodily he offered me a drink, but I declined, already having drunk several glasses of sherry.

I said in a neutral sort of voice, "What did you think of Mr Smithson's chapel."

"It's a scandal and a stumbling block," he growled. "We have heathen worship in our midst."

"That's a bit strong," I said. "Now if he had reintroduced the worship of Moloch, I should have agreed with you. But what he seems to be doing is harmless enough."

"The man's worshipping a graven image," he insisted.

I said, "Would you say the same about a Buddha?" I said.

"I certainly would," he snapped. "All images are against God's law."

"What about Our Lady?" I countered.

"That's different, man. You must see that."

"And statues of Our Lord and the saints?"

"Now that's pure obfuscation," he said, pouring himself another whisky.

"What Mr Smithson is doing is worshipping God," I said, "but he's doing it in a slightly different way from you."

"That's the most utter rubbish I've ever heard! The man's following the ancient Egyptians. Didn't you hear him? Akhenaton indeed!"

"Akhenaton was perhaps the most enlightened man of ancient times," I said, deliberately exaggerating a little.

"He was an unmitigated heathen!"

"Let's use a measure of logic," I said. "Do you agree

that any human activity which is good and loving is likely to be approved by the Almighty."

"To be sure you weren't educated by the Jesuits for nothing. Your fancy arguments won't convince me."

"Well," I said, "I can see that you do accept my statement. So if this man is basically a good man, even if his worship is slightly unorthodox, surely God will accept his offering."

"Brother Tristram, the man is worshipping a star. You know what the Holy Scriptures say about that, don't you?"

"Very well," I said, "I'll admit the man is wrong. But he is genuinely trying to use a symbol to reach God."

"There might be some excuse for those who know no better, but Mr Smithson knows all about Christ. And he has the indescribable advantage of knowing us. I think we should try to change the man's ways."

"You may if you wish," I said, "but count me out. The man is misguided but harmless. Eventually he will find the right path himself. He is at least making an effort to find God."

I tried hard to dissuade Fr O'Flynn from attempting to convert Mr Smithson, but my friend seemed determined to make the conversion of Mr Smithson his life's work. He was still at it when I left the area. He got into the habit of dropping in for a sherry every Friday night, I understand. And then they started to play chess every Friday night as well. I believe that the proportion of theological conversation on these evenings has gradually diminished to practically nothing and Mr Smithson still has his chapel with the image of the sun.

To be honest I'm still pondering the question of sun worship. I have decided that the only person who can decide what sort of worship is acceptable to God is God himself.

However, experience has taught me that God can sometimes be very cryptic. He doesn't always show his disapproval by throwing a thunderbolt at somebody. Perhaps he lets people find out for themselves.

Still, it's an ill wind that blows nobody any good. I expect Fr O'Flynn's chess has improved.

14

A thorn in the mind

Believe it or not I once fell in love with a very beautiful woman and she with me. To be truthful we were both quite young at the time. She was nineteen and I was eighteen. She was a peach. Her name was Nancy and she had flaming red hair but a sweet temper. Her face was exquisitely formed and her figure was a dream. Naturally I used to think about going to bed with her, but in those days we didn't jump into bed at the first opportunity. It was more fun, I think, to experience the joys of wondering anticipation, than to bite the cherry without a second thought.

You may ask yourself why at this time I am an elderly and celibate monk and not a happy grandfather. The answer is simple. Nancy had decided to become a nun shortly before I met her. I do not think it would be too conceited of me to remember that it was I who caused her to have second thoughts. Unhappily for my romantic dreams, she also had third thoughts which were similar to her first thoughts. She broke the news to me gently one evening when we were walking beside the river in Cambridge. She finished her degree and then shortly afterwards became Sister Veronica.

At first I thought I would commit suicide. That idea soon fizzled out when I pondered on all the joys and pleasures of this life. Then I took to drinking with some male companions and made a name for myself in the university as a tippler and woman hater. When that phase passed I tried to become a soldier but they refused to have me because I had a perforated eardrum. So what was I to do? I knew I could never fall in love with another woman. Then the answer came to me in a flash when I was sitting in church one Sunday morning. I would follow in Nancy's footsteps. I would become a monk.

It was actually much more difficult to become a monk than I had imagined. I had a spell in the navy first, the medic having omitted to perceive my perforated eardrum. Eventually, however, I persuaded the Church I had a vocation. I was trained and then finally released onto an unsuspecting world as a fledgling monk. As you know, I adopted the name Tristram and although I have not forgotten my original name I always think of myself as Tristram nowadays.

I have often pondered on this question of love. I think I am wise enough now to know that romantic love usually grows into a deeper relationship which is loving without necessarily bearing the roses of the original romantic fantasy. Of course, I love other people and like David and Jonathan have often felt a strong comradeship with another man. That sort of friendship is very comfortable and comforting. You can talk things over without being too emotionally involved with each other, unless you happen to be gay, of course. However, I have never been drawn in that direction myself, though I respect those who have.

Naturally, when I became a monk I thought a lot about Christian love and what it means. At one stage I thought I had this all sorted out in my mind. There was romantic love, there was friendship and there was Christian love. The three were clearly interrelated and it all seemed clear to me. However, I have discovered since then that life is rarely simple and that new experiences frequently challenge old opinions and prejudices.

On the question of love the challenge came to me in this way. A new Prior came to the house where I was living. I immediately took a dislike to him and he to me. He seemed to stand for everything that I loathed. He was meticulous in everything he did, but was careless about people's feelings. He preached a Gospel of punishment and I believed in a Gospel of love. He never let a matter drop but always carried it through to the bitter end. Worst of all, he never forgave anybody.

After I had known Brother Ignatius for three months I realised that my first impressions had been all too right. He was a tall thin man with iron grey hair, cut short. His rare smile was like a living lie upon his mouth, because his mind never smiled. You may think I am exaggerating. You may also think I am being uncharitable. I cannot agree with the former accusation, but I do agree with the latter. The difficulty is that Brother Ignatius and I were always like oil and water. We simply did not mix.

The man knew I disliked him. It must have showed somehow, despite my efforts to bury my antipathy. After a time he began to challenge me in all kinds of little ways. One day at table he said, "I notice, Brother Tristram, that you have missed chapel three mornings during the last month."

Everybody was looking at me. I said, "I'm sorry, Prior, I was unwell on the particular mornings you mention."

A few days later he said at our morning chapter, "Brother Tristram, why haven't you confessed to the sin of omission you committed the other day? I noticed that you did not do your share of gardening."

I said meekly, "I'm sorry, Prior, I had to do some sick visiting."

He said sniffily, "You should get yourself better organized, brother."

That sort of thing went on for some time. It was difficult, because I was bound to obey my superior. Also, I was supposed to show love to my enemies. You may think it unfair to describe Brother Ignatius as an enemy, but I'm not sure what else to call him, because his hostility became even more apparent. He criticized me publicly on

every possible occasion. He made sure I got all the difficult tasks to do. He refused every application I made to
him to do anything that was not in the normal routine of
our house. He would say, "Brother Tristram, you really
must learn to discipline yourself. You are a monk, not a
social worker."

I often found myself with clenched fists when he made
such disparaging statements. How I stopped myself from
punching him on the nose I shall never know. I was aware,
however, that any such physical reaction would be pun-
ished by the order. I would undoubtedly be given the order
of the boot.

I prayed about this relationship many times and I finally
came to the conclusion that the Lord was challenging me.
He was saying to me, "You think you know how to love,
but you have no idea. Don't you know what I felt like when
the soldiers blindfolded me and buffeted me; when the
crowd jeered at me when I was on the cross?"

I replied, "Yes, Lord, I know, but why can't you get this
man off my back. I've really tried to love him, but I can't."

The Lord replied, "It was very hard for me to love you
and all the rest of humankind, Brother Tristram. Can't you
bear a few insults for me?"

I knelt in silence for a long time. Then I said, "I'm sorry,
Lord. I'm not up to it. I'm going to ask for a transfer."

Such a move was allowed in certain circumstances. It
meant I would have to have an interview with the General
of the order. I had to obtain permission for this interview
through Brother Ignatius. When I went to ask him for such
an interview his lip curled with a supercilious smile of
triumph. He knew he had driven me out. And I knew that I
had failed in my vocation.

It was many years before I became comfortable with
this episode in my life. I concluded that the Lord knew I
would fail and that he wanted to take me beyond my limits
so that I wouldn't judge other people too harshly. That has

certainly been the effect of Brother Ignatius's influence on my life. I know what failure is like and I try not to judge other people for their failures. However, I still can't bring myself to be merciful in my thoughts about Brother Ignatius. That is a thorn the Lord has given to me.

15

Vandal of the spirit

I suppose it could be claimed that the composition of grafiti is an art form. Certainly I have seen some interesting examples, some of them witty, or even poetic. One grafito I read while relieving myself once in a London lavatory read:

Madge is marvellous to lay
I lie and think of her all day
until its (sic) time to hit the hay
with Madge the girl I like to lay.

While this is not exactly Dantesque, there is a certain sincerity about the verse which appeals to me. However, as it was written in the wrong place it certainly has to be classified as an example of vandalism.

I often wonder if history has perpetrated an injustice on the Vandals by associating their name with desecration. Surely some of them had an interest in the creative arts? My theory is supported by the historical fact that when they sacked Rome the Vandals took away with them quite a lot of works of art. It is possible, of course, that they wished to sell them, but there is a little corner of my heart which hopes that they enjoyed them for their own sake.

Did you know that in the United States there is a town called Vandalia? Presumably this unfortunate township is either named after the Finnish town of Vanda or more hopefully after a beautiful orchid of the same name.

You may think that I'm chattering on a little. However, I was really thinking of the time when a picture of Our Lady was vandalised in a parish church while I was working there. It was a very beautiful picture. I arrived at the church for mass one morning when I found a small crowd gathered round the picture. I walked across and saw, to my consternation, that someone had scratched all over Our Lady's face with a sharp instrument. I guessed that it was beyond repair.

People were naturally speculating as to the identity of the vandal, but nobody seemed able to come up with a solution. It was very difficult to understand what motive could lie behind the destruction of the picture. My own view was that somebody had a grudge against the church in general or against Our Lady in particular, perhaps because of an unanswered prayer. Anyway, we went on with mass and as would be expected we prayed for the person who had destroyed the picture.

That event was destined to remain one of life's unsolved mysteries. However, it illustrates how desperate people can feel sometimes. Perhaps the guilty person "murdered" the picture instead of his wife, in which case I imagine Our Lady would be thankful that she had been instrumental in preventing a murder. I have always been a sympathiser with the "but for the grace of God" school of thought, because I am all too aware of my own human weakness. However, there was a much more worrying case of vandalism while I worked in the same parish. I suppose you could call it an example of spiritual vandalism. What I mean is that somebody deliberately tried to destroy the spirituality of the congregation.

The only person who has the power to destroy a congregation's faith is the priest in charge of the parish. This was the case at St Benedict's and the unthinkable began to happen when Fr Dieteralli was appointed to the parish. I had been looking after things since Fr Medici had left three months previously, and I believe the parish was in good spiritual order when I handed it over.

Fr Dieteralli, I believe, had an Italian grandfather and an

Irish grandmother. His parents, however, had been brought up in Scotland and had moved to England just before Fr Dieteralli was born. His parents were Scottish in outlook and accent, though Fr Dieteralli himself was thoroughly English, having attended a famous Catholic public school before training as a priest.

After he had been our priest for about a month I began to notice certain worrying tendencies in him. His sermons were challenging and even heretical in some respects. It was as if he was questioning the very existence of God, having a dialogue between the priest and the doubter within himself. That in itself is not a unique happening, but there was a consistency in this man's attacks upon the divinity which was startling. Then I heard by devious means that he had been giving some strange advice in the confessional and even swearing at people. Then he started to quarrel with people, first with the organist over the choice of hymns; and then with the parish sister; and then with me and numerous other people. There was a trail of destruction in personal relationships and trust in the parish which was difficult to believe.

Loyalty to a fellow priest made me reluctant to take any action. I concluded at first that he was having a hard time with his own faith and that this was showing more than it should have done. However, when he went berserk in front of the Sunday School I felt I had to remonstrate with him. What he did was to tear a strip off a young girl who was a teacher in the Sunday School and all she had done was to forget to bring her copy of the Bible story for the day.

That same evening I went to see Fr Dieteralli. He growled at me: "What the hell do you want?"

I said, "Just a quiet word, Anthony, if I may."

"It's extremely inconvenient. I was just going to have my supper. But if you make it snappy you can come in."

When we had sat down in his study I said, "Didn't you go over the top a bit this morning?"

"Why don't you mind your own bloody business?" he snapped.

"It is my business," I said firmly, "especially when I see a fellow priest destroying a parish."

"What do you know about it? You're not a parish priest."

We went on sparring for some time, but I couldn't get through to him. I reluctantly left the matter there for the time being.

Over the next three months things went from bad to worse. The congregation was halved. Many parents kept their children away from Sunday School. Above all, gossip was rife. Mainly the talk was about Fr Anthony's past. All kinds of rumours circulated about the wicked deeds he was supposed to have done. I tried to control this gossip as best I could, but I know it continued. You can always tell when people are huddling in little groups after mass that they are talking about some serious issue. The matter came to a head when a round robin letter was written to the bishop.

The bishop called to see me first, before going to Fr Anthony. He has a way with him, the bishop, and he managed to prise out of me bit by bit what was going on in the parish. When he left he said, "Not a word to anyone. Leave things to me."

The next thing everybody knew Fr Dieteralli left the parish. That left me in charge again. I can tell you there were lots of broken pieces to pick up.

It was some time before I saw the bishop again. I plucked up courage to ask him where Fr Dieteralli was now. The bishop said, "I'm afraid the poor man is in an institution for the mentally disturbed."

I risked a rap on the knuckles by asking, "What was wrong with him, then?"

The bishop looked at me appraisingly. Then he said, "I suppose you deserve some sort of explanation because you have borne the brunt of the damage. Anthony Dieteralli was virtually forced into the priesthood by his parents against his wishes. Ever since he has borne a grudge against them and the whole church. I really do wish parents would seek advice about vocations. I'm sure this should have been spotted years ago. In the meantime, goodness knows what damage has been done."

As I said earlier, Anthony Dieteralli's actions were a form of spiritual vandalism. However, his story is a good example of how a fuller knowledge of a person makes it possible to understand and even condone his actions. I'm sure a lot of vandalism is committed in reaction to spiritual or physical violence against the person concerned. It worries me a lot more on the rare occasion when the violence of the vandal does not have any explanation, but seems to arise from some devilish and mischievous source. I have only met one person in that category, but that is another story.

16

The generation cliff

My work has permitted me to be involved in the personal problems of many different people from all walks of life. I remember the case of a young girl who had run away from home because she couldn't get along with her parents. She was an only child and the parents were naturally very upset.

I was talking to the girl's father a few days after she had absonded. He said angrily, "It's all theChurch's fault. Whatever happened to the teaching about honouring your parents? If Moira had been taught that properly when she was a child she wouldn't have run off."

Jim's wife, Eileen, came into the room at that point. She had obviously overheard what her husband had said. She shouted, "Don't be so blasphemous about the Church, our Jim. It's all your fault for being so hard on the girl."

The two then went over what I took to be a well rehearsed argument while I sat in silence sipping a cup of tea. The gist of the argument was that Jim thought his wife had been too easy with the girl from the time she was very small, while his wife thought he had been too heavy handed all through the girl's life. The issue that had driven the girl away was whether or not she could share a flat with a girl friend. However, Moira was only just eighteen and she was somewhat immature. I knew the girl because she was in the local church choir.

When the argument had subsided I said, "Do you know where Moira has gone?"

Jim explained that their daughter had left a note, but no

forwarding address. The police had refused to act because the girl was of an age to make up her own mind.

I then said, "Who is the girl she was going to share with?"

"Emma Smith," said Eileen. "I've been to see her and her parents, but they won't say where Moira's gone. But I'm sure they know."

It so happened that I was due a few days vacation, so I said, "Would you like me to try to find Moira?"

Eileen said, "Would you, Brother Tristram? We would be ever so grateful."

Jim grunted, which I took as a sign of agreement. I said, "I have to say that I am not willing to put any pressure on Moira to come back. But I will talk to her. Where does she work?"

"That's the trouble," said Jim. "She's left and they can't say where she's gone either, though I think they know."

It wasn't difficult to find the girl. Emma Smith's parents told me readily enough where Moira was when I promised not to tell her parents without the girl's permission.

The next evening I went along to the address they had given me. It was a big house, but Moira had rented only one room and had to share a bathroom and kitchen with numerous other tenants, most of them students. She was at home. When she opened her door she reluctantly invited me in. She did not ask me to sit down, so I sat on the edge of the bed.

There are some words I cannot bring myself to record on paper, so you must excuse some of the gaps in my account of our conversation. It's not that I've never heard the words before. In fact, when I served in the navy I knew a petty officer who used much more colourful language. Anyway, when I sat down she said, "What do you want you ... old fool?"

I said, "Just a chat."

"My parents ... well sent you. Well, you can go back and tell them that I'm not ... well coming home."

"I have no intention of trying to persuade you to return home," I said. "I just wanted to check that you are safe."

"I've heard about you bloody ... monks," she said. "If you think you're going to get into my bed to...you're mistaken."

I was quite amused by that idea, I must say. She was a singularly unattractive girl with prominent teeth and skinny legs. However, not a ghost of a smile appeared on my lips. I said, "Not everybody's perfect, including you. Why don't you tell me what all the trouble is about? It might help to talk things over with an old fool like me."

At that she burst out laughing. "You're not stuck up, are you?"

I thought it wiser to wait for her to go on. After a pause she said, "All I wanted to do was share a flat with my mate. Lots of girls do it."

"Were there any boys to share?" I said, suspecting that there might be other dimensions to the problem.

"What if there were?" she said. "Nowadays people live together without going to bed you know."

"It would worry your parents, though, wouldn't it. They remember when they were young you see, and they know how tempting it is to go to bed with somebody."

"Not my parents," she said sarcastically. "They never had any temptations like that, I assure you."

"I can assure you that they did," I said. "Everybody does."

"Well there weren't going to be any boys," she said. "Just Emma and me. Not that we're lesbian, mind you – though I might have a go at that one day."

She obviously still thought I was shockable so I said, "Some of my best friends are lesbians. But anyway, I have an idea. If I can persuade your parents to agree to you and

Emma living together, will you promise to visit them at least once every week?"

"You haven't a ... hope," she said. "My dad's so obstinate he would make a mule look like a push over."

"I have my ways," I said. "I think I might just be able to persuade him. It's your dad, not your mum, isn't it?"

"Right first time. O.K. I'll agree to that. Otherwise it's no go."

I went back to see Jim and Eileen as promised. I decided it would be wise to prepare the ground a little before revealing my master plan. I explained that I had found Moira and that she was well, but that I didn't have any hope at all of persuading her to come back.

Then I said, "Jim, you remember when you talked about that bit of the Bible which talks about honouring parents?"

"I certainly do," he said. "It doesn't happen nowadays, does it?"

"Every coin has two sides, you know."

"How do you mean?" he said.

"If parents honour and respect their children, then they will in turn honour and respect their parents."

He was silent and his face was grim. However, Eileen said, "I see what you mean. Yes I do. Don't you Jim?"

"Children should be kept in their place," he said.

I said, "It's quite likely you'll never see your daughter again if you don't change your attitude."

"What am I supposed to do?" he growled. "She's still a kid."

"That's not the impression I got," I said. "But listen, if Moira would agree to come to see you at least once a week, would you agree to let her live with Emma. It seems a harmless enough arrangement to me."

Eileen wisely remained silent. Her husband thought for a while and then said, "I suppose we could give it try."

I said, "I'll see what I can do. By the way, is there a

cup of tea going? I seem to have developed a great thirst."

Eileen smiled at me. "Are you sure you wouldn't prefer something stronger, Brother Tristram?"

"I never argue with a lady," I said.

17
The gossiping angel

I was talking to an angel one day. I happened to meet him when I was walking late at night along a country road. If you want to know what an angel looks like, I can't tell you, because it was fairly dark at the time. All I can say is that this one didn't fly down from heaven. He was walking in the opposite direction when I met him. I was just slightly worried when I saw this shape gliding towards me, but when he was about five yards away he called to me in a cheerful voice, "Is that you, Brother Tristram? I thought I might meet you along this road."

The voice was friendly enough, but I didn't recognize it. I said, "Who are you?"

He said, "That's not important. The important question is 'Who are you?'"

"That's a silly question," I said. "You've just told me who I am."

"But who is Brother Tristram? What kind of a person is he?"

"A fairly ordinary sort of bloke," I said. I couldn't think of anything else to say.

By this time the angel was walking beside me. He said, "Tell me, Brother Tristram, are you a righteous man?"

"That's a terrible question to ask a man at this time of day," I said. "Why couldn't you ask me when I was saying my prayers this morning?"

"So you think you're more righteous when you're saying your prayers?" he said, a sarcastic edge to his voice.

"Well, it stands to reason, doesn't it," I replied, slightly annoyed. "When a man's saying his prayers that's when he's closest to God."

"Righteousness isn't like that, Brother Tristram, and you know perfectly well it isn't."

"I do know it's a hard thing to be," I said. "The trouble is if you think you're righteous you probably aren't, because you're self righteous."

"I like that, Brother Tristram. Yes, I like it. But what I'm asking you to do is to tell me what you think righteousness is. And if you can do that I'll save your blushes and tell you whether you are righteous or not."

"Surely it's a moral concept," I said. "The opposite is unrighteousness, and if you're like that, as most of us are, then you're a sinner. So it's the opposite of being a sinner."

"Not good enough, I'm afraid, Brother... may I call you Tristram?"

"If you like," I said. "But why don't you tell me what it is then, if you're so fussy."

"I'm not the one who's fussy," he said. "It's the Boss. Suppose he sends for you tonight, can you stand before him and say, 'I am a righteous man.'"

"Don't be silly," I said. "Nobody can do that. Nobody except one person, I mean."

"Oh, you mean the Boss himself? Well, that must be right of course. But there are degrees of righteousness. You can be eighty percent righteous, for example. So, let me rephrase the question. What percentage would you score on the righteousness machine?"

"At a guess," I said, "I should say fifty percent. You see, I know I'm half bad and half good."

"Very good," he said, laughing merrily. "But which half is good and which half is bad. Are you bad from the waist down, or is the right half of you bad?"

"You're winding me up," I said. "You know I didn't mean that."

"Let me ask you a different question then, Tristram.

Suppose you were asked to judge whether another person was righteous, how would you set about it?"

"You're trying to trap me," I said. "Whatever I say you'll throw it back at me."

"We aren't like that," he said. "Go on, have a go!"

"Very well," I said. "A righteous person would keep the law of God. Mainly he would love his neighbour."

"You got that out of the Good Book," he complained. "That's cheating. I want your own opinion."

"Hang about," I said. "I thought the Bible was supposed to guide everybody."

"So it is. But you are supposed to be a trained theologian. I don't expect ready made answers from you now, do I?"

I sighed. "Very well then. A person has to be filled with goodness and love from tip to toe. Is that personal enough for you?"

"Go on," he said.

"The result of that would be that the person concerned would drive out sin because there wouldn't be any room for it. Then he would be nearly righteous."

"You are cautious tonight. Why 'nearly'?"

"It stands to reason. Human beings aren't perfect."

"Very well," said the angel. "Now you aren't going to like what I'm going to say next."

"I knew you were going to throw it back at me," I said furiously.

The angel laughed. "No, not at all. You're going to throw it back at yourself. What I was going to say was, 'I think you really are righteous.' What do you say to that?"

"You knew all the time what I was thinking about," I said. "You know perfecty well that I hate two people with all my heart. You know I'm not righteous. Why are you tormenting me?"

When I looked round the angel had gone. However, he had made his point. I decided I'd better do something about the two people I didn't like very much. It was hard to think

82

of the right thing to do, but I decided eventually that I would ask each of them to spend a day with me. Separately, of course. I would take each of them out to lunch and I would listen politely when they said things I disagreed with.

I can tell you, it's an uncomfortable business talking to angels.

18

My friend Jimmy

I have only ever been in hospital once as a patient. However, it was for a lengthy stay. My enforced rest lasted for twelve months and I fear I was something of a trial to those around me. Fortitude has never been my strong suit. Mind you, up to that time I had always fancied I could inspire others to fortitude, but when it came to practising what I preached I'm afraid I was an abject failure.

For the first fortnight I was a model patient, but I believed then that I was only going to be in hospital for about three weeks. Anybody can show fortitude over a short period. However, the specialist came along one day and said, "Brother Tristram, the treatment for your collapsed lung doesn't seem to be working. It looks as if you will have to have the operation."

This was a shock. I had been assured that the pipe that had been inserted between my ribs would gradually pump all the air outside my lung into the large bottle it was attached to. I must say that it was very inconvenient to be joined to a large bottle all the time, but it was supposed to be a short term measure that would cure my condition. I was suffering from what is called spontaneous lung collapse. For no apparent reason my left lung had shrunk to half its size. This change had been indicated to me by an almost unbearable pain in the middle of my chest. My brothers had immediately called an ambulance, thinking I was having a heart attack. Before I was put into the ambulance I was given an injection. Whatever the substance was that then coursed through my veins, it had a terrifying effect. Every few seconds my limbs were jerked by sudden spasms. These were painless, but nevertheless unnerving. Before I reached the hospital the pain in my chest had subsided. It was three days before it was discovered that my heart was as sound as a bell. An X ray had revealed that my lung had collapsed.

The surgeon had said, "Don't worry, old chap. We can deal with these things without any problem."

At that he gave me what was supposed to be a local anaesthetic and shoved a knife between my ribs. Two other doctors held me down while this was going on behind a screen. The other patients in the ward must have concluded I was being murdered because I have never been one to suffer physical pain in silence.

After three weeks with my pet bottle, a further X ray showed that my lung had not inflated at all. The surgeon then made a further cheerful and incorrect prediction: "Don't worry, old chap. These chest operations are a piece of cake nowadays."

I'm afraid that from then on I ceased to be anything like a model patient. The ward sister made a throw away re-mark which didn't help. She said, "The doctor's going to give the bottle another week to work. If it doesn't, then you'll have to have the operation. Let's hope it doesn't come to that. Chest operations are very painful afterwards, you know."

I was not amused when the nurse arrived to shave me the night before the operation. I have never been able to fathom why it is necessary to shave off all hair between the knees and the neck for a chest operation. Did the doctor think he might have to operate, while he was at it, some-where in the lower regions? Was there something the doc-tor hadn't told me?

The sister's prediction was more accurate than the sur-geon's. Recovery from the operation was a slow and pain-ful process. There were various complications which I won't go into, but the fact is that septicaemia set in and when that was cured another operation was found to be necessary. Month followed after month and it seemed to me that I was never going to be released from that hospital.

I soon became the oldest resident of the ward, in the sense that I had been there the longest. People came and went at a rapid rate. It was at first quite painful to lose newly made friends as they achieved their desired cures and then cheerfully went off home. Then I became used to the rites of passage through the ward. I came to know precisely what people would say when they came to wish me goodbye. They always promised to come back to see me, but they never did.

After I had been in the ward for about five months a young boy arrived. He was due to have a new plastic valve fitted into his heart. This was his third time. He was extraordinarily cheerful and I took to him immediately. In fact, he made me feel ashamed of myself and I became much less cantankerous. Jimmy, his name was. I can't for the life of me remember his surname.

As it turned out complications set in for Jimmy and he stayed in hospital much longer than was anticipated. We soon cemented a strong friendship and we were put into adjacent beds. When Jimmy first discovered I was a monk this put a strain on our relationship, but he gradually got used to the idea and our friendship became stronger than ever. He even joined with me in my prayers every evening.

Whatever calamities happened to Jimmy he remained as cheerful as ever. Altogether he had three operations on top of those he had had previously. He and his parents at last believed that the sequence of cutting and binding was over and the boy was beginning to think of going home. I was feeling rather sad at the prospect of separation. However, one morning, Jimmy seemed not to be as cheerful as usual. He was very pale and he seemed to be in pain. At first he asked me not to tell the nurse. I could see he was afraid that his home going might be delayed. However, I finally persuaded him to let me inform the ward sister.

Shortly afterwards a doctor rushed in. The curtains were drawn round Jimmy's bed. There were whispered consultations. Then a stretcher and a trolley were brought and the boy was taken away. I questioned the nurses and they told me Jimmy was in a side ward. I was told that it would be impossible for me to go and see him. Three days later I heard he had died.

This event almost destroyed my morale. However, it was Jimmy himself who was my inspiration and I managed to hold together. The boy's parents came in to see me before they left the hospital for the final time. His mother was too upset to say anything. However, his father thanked me for all the help I was supposed to have given to his son. I said quietly, "I can assure you that Jimmy helped me a lot more than I helped him. But one thing I'm sure of, he has gone straight to heaven."

I suppose the Lord speaks to us in many different ways. As far as I was concerned God's word came to me very strongly through my friendship with that young boy. He was with me in spirit for the rest of my stay in hospital and his fortitude somehow gave me much more patience to accept my own experience of adversity. His was a great soul and despite his youth I know he was much further on the pilgrimage towards God than I am.

19

How I came by a white cat

I have never encountered perfect goodness during my life, so far anyway, except I suppose in God. At the same time I have never met complete wickedness. However, I have met people closely approaching perfection and completeness respectively in these opposing categories.

Mrs Evelyn Hodgson was an elderly lady who lived in an old terraced house in a quiet side street. I knew her from church and I had come to respect her greatly. She had been a widow for very many years, having lost her husband in the war. She was a small lady with a very engaging smile and a charming manner. She also did many good works in her own modest and unassuming way. Once when she was sick I took communion to her house. That was how I came to be one of her friends. After that I used to call regularly, always being sure of a warm and loving welcome, not only from Evelyn, but also from her white cat, Thompson. I understand she called the cat Thompson after an old friend of hers. As she explained, "I couldn't call him Mary, because of his sex, so I settled for Thompson. He seems quite happy with his name."

I'm sure he was, because he was more than happy with the person who gave it to him.

Evelyn had no children, but she had a nephew called Neville. He was a car salesman and very smooth. When I say smooth I mean as smooth as a snake in the grass. Oddly enough, Evelyn never mentioned Neville to me until one day I called when he happened to be there. As a matter of fact I heard a snatch of conversation through the window just before I rang the door bell. It was so shocking that I delayed ringing the bell for a moment or so in order to hear more. I know that is supposed to be ill mannered, but in some circumstances loving care overrules good manners.

I heard Emily say, "Your mother wouldn't like it, Neville."

"She's bloody dead and gone, you old fool, a pile of ashes at the crem. So what about it? I need the money."

"I'll see what I can do," said Evelyn.

At that point I rang the door bell. When Evelyn opened the door she looked slightly flustered. Her face was red and her eyes rather swollen. However, she said in her usual cheerful way, "Come in, Brother Tristram."

I said, "Are you sure it's convenient? Perhaps I could come back another time."

"You're welcome any time," she said. "Come and meet my nephew. He's my sister's boy."

To describe Neville as a boy was pushing it a bit. He was in his mid forties, I guessed. He had sleek black hair with a moustache to match and he was wearing a smart brown suit. My first impression was of oiliness. His handshake was a bit sticky and his manner slick.

"Good afternoon," he said, smiling like a tiger just about to snatch his prey. "I see you're a man of the cloth. I'm afraid I'm a lost soul. And as far as I'm concerned the church is a lost cause."

Evelyn said quickly, "Neville was just going."

"Don't worry, Auntie. I shan't upset the man. He knows there are lots of sinners like me around. I'll be in touch."

"Very well, dear. I'll think over what you said."

Neville did not reply, but he gave Evelyn a stare which would have turned Genghis Khan to stone. She gave a startled look, like a rabbit surprised by a stoat. Neville left without another word. Evelyn did not go to the door with him.

After a pause I said, "Is everything all right, Evelyn?"

"Of course," she said. "Tea or coffee?"

Thompson stalked into the room at that point and miaowed plaintively. Evelyn said, "So what would you like, my lovely? A saucer of milk from mummy?"

I chatted to Evelyn for half an hour and then I left to visit a sick parishioner.

About a fortnight later I called to see Evelyn again. To my consternation she had a black eye. She said she had bumped into a door, but I could see she was lying. That woman was so intrinsically innocent and good that she couldn't lie easily. It went against her nature.

A few weeks later I called again. Through the window I heard a man's voice shouting. However, when I went into the living room everything seemed normal. Neville gave almost a repeat performance of his conversation the last time I saw him and he departed just as quickly, looking slightly shifty.

I hoped that any trouble that had been brewing for Evelyn had simmered down. However, the next time I called, Evelyn was bent over in pain when she opened the door. She claimed she had a grumbling appendix, but I had seen Neville's posh car disappearing round the corner as I arrived and I drew my own conclusions.

Ten days later the parish priest knocked on my door and told me that Evelyn Hodgson was dead. He knew few details, but apparently an intruder had bludgeoned her to death and stolen her ready cash. I was naturally horrified when I thought of that dear old lady meeting such a fate. When further details emerged I was even more horrified because her assailant had struck her innumerable times with a heavy brass ornament which normally stood on her mantelpiece. I remembered the ornament well because she had told me that her only sister, now dead, had left it to her in her will. It didn't occur to me at the time that Neville, the dead sister's son, might have perpetrated this evil deed.

The police made extensive enquiries but had not been

able to make an arrest after three months of enquiry. The only finger prints found in the house were Evelynl's own, mine, a neighbour's and her nephew's. Each of us was automatically ruled out because of our friendly relationship with Evelyn. However, Neville started splashing his money around when it seemed that he was in the clear. Most people believed that Evelyn had not had much money, but what she had possessed she had kept under the mattress. This is obviously a very unimaginative place to keep money, because any half intelligent thief would look there first. Nobody knew for certain how much money she had saved, but her neighbour claimed that it was certainly over ten thousand pounds, because Evelyn had told her about it one day in case she was called suddenly to meet her Maker. Poor Evelyn. She had not realised exactly in what circumstances she would meet the Almighty.

One day somebody mentioned to a friend of a friend of a policeman that Neville seemed to have come into some money. The police then renewed their enquiries and one afternoon a detective came to interview me. He asked particularly about Neville and if I had ever seen him at Evelyn's house. I told him exactly what I have told you. Then it turned out that the good neighbour had a few horror stories to tell about Neville. Furthermore, Neville could give no satisfactory explanation as to how he had obtained the money he was spending so freely. He told several stories in explanation, but each of them turned out to be false.

I was called as a witness at Neville's trial for the murder of his aunt. While he was in court he looked just as smooth as he always did. He told a farrago of lies, but was trapped several times by the prosecuting counsel. In the end he admitted he had murdered Evelyn. He also said in a flat voice, "She was asking for it. If it hadn't been me it would have been somebody else. She was just a silly old woman who would have died anyway at the drop of a hat."

Neville showed no remorse either then, or later. I did visit him once in prison, but he indicated very clearly that he did not wish to see me again.

One of the ironies of the case was that in her will Evelyn had left her money and the brass ornament to Neville. She left Thompson in my care and I was very glad to accept that responsibility.

I have often wondered whether a death penalty would have deterred Neville from murdering Evelyn, but somehow I doubt it. He was simply a bad lot. Having said that, I still stick to my belief that every human being is on a pilgrimage to God. In the case of Neville and others like him, I can only imagine that somewhere, somehow, they are going to have some very painful experiences before they can make any progress up the ladder of grace. On the other hand, I have no doubt that Evelyn is at this very moment praying for the welfare of her nephew.

20

How a long dead dragon fly
spoke to me

I learned when I was about nine years old that there is a
difference between wanting something that belongs to somebody else and wanting something that you get by your own
efforts. I remember that my cousin, who was also nine
years old at the time, possessed a wonderful collection of
fossils. One of them was a beauty and I wanted it more than
anything in the world. It was a piece of amber containing a
small dragon fly. I dreamed about possessing that particular fossil night after night. At last the temptation to take the
fossil surreptitiously from my cousin's collection became
too much. I knew it might be a while before it was missed
and I did not believe that my cousin would suspect I had
taken it.

When I had stolen this precious jewel it somehow seemed
to lose its charm. I still had dreams about it, but they were
nightmarish. Hordes of dragon flies haunted my sleep and
they kept jumping out of pieces of amber and biting me.
After five days I put the fossil back where it belonged. A
great weight was lifted off my mind. I almost decided to
confess my theft to my cousin, but discretion was the better
part of valour and I remained silent.

The slightly odd sequel was that my cousin went off to
prep school as a boarder a few months later. Before he
went he told me that he was tired of collecting fossils and
asked me if I would like to have his collection. Well, I have
never been one to look a gift horse in the mouth, so I
accepted gratefully, but to ease my still prickly conscience
I gave him my shiny stone. This was a most valuable
possession and it was a great sacrifice to part with it. It was

almost perfectly spherical and it had purple and green veins spreading over a red background. My cousin was in transports of delight when I gave it to him, so I felt I had wiped the slate clean.

Many years later I met a man who was having a similar experience to mine, though it concerned much more valuable property. Actually, he came to ask my advice about this matter one day while I was examining my now huge collection of fossils. Consequently, when he told me his story the parallel was very much in my mind.

When Victor Gadogan arrived I invited him into my study and offered him a glass of sherry. I knew him slightly because we had worked together on a project for orphaned children. I had no idea at the time that he was a church person like myself. We chatted for a while about the project we had worked on and then I said, "What can I do for you, Victor?"

He said, "I have a problem of conscience, Brother Tristram."

"Would you like to tell me about it? I assume that is why you have come."

"Yes. I need to get something off my chest. I would appreciate another opinion. You see, my cousin is the managing director of our family firm. I'm the secretary, but naturally I wish to progress. In a way I suppose it's about wanting my cousin's job, but I have never thought about it seriously until recently. I discovered by accident two months ago that my cousin is cheating the firm. It's not a small amount that's involved. He's milking the profits over and above his salary to the extent of about ten thousand pounds a year. Now the thing is, I could shop him and take over his job. I'm sure I would be the natural choice of the other directors. The trouble is I'm having dreams every night about being the boss and it's taking over my whole life."

"What is the alternative?" I said.

"I could face my cousin with the situation and offer to

94

help him to put things right. I suppose it could be done. In any case, there's no question of involving the police. My fellow directors would wish to hush up the situation if I told them about it and my cousin would be put out to grass. He's got enough money to survive without discomfort."

One of my principles in advising people usually is to let them make up their own minds, but in this case I was led to slant my advice in a particular way because of the child-hood experience I have just recounted. Perhaps this is an example of God's providence. I have found in my life that past experiences are rarely ever wasted. So, I said, "Victor, it's fairly clear to me that you would have a very prickly conscience if you shopped your cousin. The glorious attractions of being the boss would crumble to dust as soon as you were promoted. My advice would be to face your cousin with the truth, but offer to help him out. What he then does is up to him. If he accepts your offer and continues he may be a much better man because of your compassion. On the other hand, if he resigns, using some other pretext as an excuse, that would leave the way open for you to become the managing director with your conscience clear."

He said, "It's amazing how an objective view clears away the impenetrable jungle in a problem. Things are now absolutely crystal clear. I shall take your advice."

I didn't explain to Victor how I knew what the right action should be. After all, a man doesn't throw away his reputation for wisdom lightly. However, I give God the credit in this case, because I'm sure he sent Victor on purpose just at the time I was looking over my fossils. Did I tell you that I had the amber one containing the dragon fly in my hand when Victor rang the door bell?

Victor came to see me again a few weeks later. He explained that his cousin had resigned from the firm on the grounds of ill health and that he, Victor, had been offered his cousin's job. Victor asked me if he could do something for me in return. I said, "I'm not allowed to accept things, but the monastery I belong to is building a home for the handicapped."

A few days later Victor sent me a very fat cheque. It was accompanied by a letter headed with the firm's name and the name of the new managing director in large letters. I have my own little vanities so I did not feel too critical of Victor for showing off his new prize.

21

The bells of heaven

I was wondering the other day what it would be like to be thrown to the lions. Human cruelty takes many forms, and perhaps there are worse fates than being mauled and eaten by a lion. Certainly, it can be supposed that once a lion has made up its mind to kill you it is not going to take long about it. Possibly the worst part of being a meal for a lion is knowing beforehand for several days that your fate is to be just that. I suppose the early Christians who were martyred in this way must have pondered whether it was worth dying for a religious cause. The temptation to give up the Christian faith must have been great.

I expect you are a bit puzzled yourself as to why an elderly monk should be exercising his brain on such a question. It would seem a little unlikely that anyone would decide to throw me to the lions. Moreover, I suspect a lion would find me too stringy to be a very appetising meal. That is by the way. I can, in fact, tell you confidentially that my train of thought was started by the recent imprisonment of a former colleague of mine in a South American country. Like the early Christians he was imprisoned because of his religious faith, not because he had committed any crime.

Naturally I prayed for my friend, Brother St Michael, as did many other people. After quite a lot of prayer I began to wonder where it was all leading to. Then I remembered something a famous person once said. Before I tell you what it was he said, perhaps I can just say that I often find the sayings of famous people difficult to understand. I have come to the conclusion that I must be an obtuse sort of person. Anyway, the person whose words I remembered was no less than God's Son, so I suppose it is to be expected that he would say and do some fairly startling things.

Jesus of Nazareth, of course, was himself persecuted, so he knew a lot about the subject. Also, he must have known that his followers would be persecuted and that is possibly why he said that the persecuted would be blessed. Moreover he said that the kingdom of heaven would be theirs. I happen to know just a little Greek so I had a peek at this saying in my Greek Bible, even though my Greek is rusty. Not that Jesus spoke Greek, you understand, but it seems that the record of what he said came down to us in Greek, so that is as near to the fountainhead as you can get. I won't trouble you with the Greek, but I am assured that a fairly accurate version in English of what the Son of God said about persecution would be as follows: "Those who are persecuted for the sake of righteousness are blessed, because theirs is the kingdom of heaven."

I puzzled over these words for a long time. I wondered what Brother St Michael thought about them, because I'm sure they must have come into his mind when he was put into gaol. All I could think of were phrases like "Pie in the sky" and "Promises, promises!"

Then one day I was having a cup of tea and a piece of Victoria sponge cake with Sister Ursula and she said, "What news is there about Brother St Michael?"

I felt terrible, I can tell you. There was I scoffing sponge cake and chatting cheerily to an old friend and all the time my Brother in Christ was suffering in a filthy prison. I had to force down the rest of the cake so as not to offend Sister Ursula, but I can tell you that it almost choked me.

When I had swallowed a mouthful of cake I said, "The British ambassador has been to see him. Apparently the authorities won't budge. They claim Brother St Michael has been instigating rebellion and treason by preaching about freedom in Christ."

"I always did wonder about all that liberation theology," she said. "Now look where it's got him."

"That's hardly fair," I said. "He's preaching a practical Gospel, that's all."

"He can't do much preaching where he is," she said.

"Surely he's acting out the Gospel by being in prison," I said. "But anyway, I've been giving the matter a lot of thought, especially in relation to the idea of the persecuted being in heaven. It's a difficult saying that, don't you think so?"

"I don't see what's difficult about it," she said. "It stands to reason that if you are persecuted for Christ you go to heaven when you die."

"What about the kingdom of heaven now?" I said. "It's all very well going through absolute hell, but what about those who never suffer for Christ at all. Some people go to church every Sunday and then go home to roast beef and Yorkshire pudding. They expect to go to heaven as well."

"Don't you have roast beef and Yorkshire pudding every Sunday?" she said crisply.

Sister Ursula has the habit of hitting the nail right of the head. In a blinding flash I saw what my difficulty was. I was actually jealous of Brother St Michael because he was truly suffering for his faith, whereas providence had always guided me beside still waters and into green pastures.

She said, "Have another piece of cake."

I hesitated and then thought to myself, "Refusing a piece of cake isn't going to help anybody."

After I have finished that piece of cake I said, "Have you ever been persecuted, Sister Ursula?"

"What are you getting at now, you silly man? Of course I haven't."

"Doesn't that worry you?" I said.

She smiled in a kindly sort of way. "I can see what your

trouble is. You still want to be a hero for the faith, don't you."

I blushed and muttered, "I have a guilty conscience."

She said, "Brother St Michael is doing what he has been called to do. So are you. But don't think you've got away with anything. Some time, in this life or the next, Christ will ask of you everything you've got. Then you'll know what it's all about. As for the persecuted being in the kingdom of heaven now, well in a sense they must be. God is everywhere, so his kingdom must be everywhere, even in Brother Michael's prison. Have another piece of cake?"

That last piece of cake on the plate suddenly seemed enormously delicious and tempting. My teeth craved to bite into it. But my tongue said, "No thank you." My mind said, "You can't transport that piece of cake to Brother St Michael, so it makes no difference to him whether you eat it or not."

Sister Ursula said, "Perhaps the politicians will intervene to release Brother St Michael."

Sadly that proved not to be the case. He was executed for treason about ten days after my conversation with Sister Ursula. I think about him a lot. Sometimes I conclude in my meditations that he gave his life away for nothing. At other times I think that perhaps every time somebody suffers for a right or a principle, a bell rings in heaven to tell everybody that another saint is about to arrive.

I can only hope that the next life contains fewer mysteries and uncertainties than this one. Sister Ursula seems to have fewer problems than I do in the face of these metaphysical puzzles. Still, as I said, I must be an obtuse sort of person.

22

A question of perspective

Most of us have split personalities. This is particularly true of myself when I compare my behaviour as a driver with my behaviour as a pedestrian. While I am driving the car all pedestrians are dangerous lunatics. However, as soon as I step out of the car and walk along the road all drivers turn into potential monsters.

Of course this kind of role reversal is true in larger matters. An old friend of mine, now sadly long departed this life, was a chaplain in the armed forces during the Second World War. A man who had been a fellow student of his at the seminary became a chaplain on the opposing side to my friend. Joe, as my friend was called, managed to remain in contact with the other chaplain through the good offices of a Spanish priest. At the same time, each chaplain was praying ardently for his own side. Naturally, Joe and his friend Karl were aware of the contradictions in this nationalistic form of worship. However, the two chaplains remained friends even though they were officially designated as enemies.

It is sometimes difficult to identify the person who initially starts a dispute, whether it is a war or a quarrel between neighbours. Once the aggro starts it builds up until sometimes the original cause of the argument is forgotten and the protagonists are simply giving knee jerk responses to the latest aggravation by the other side. That reminds me, in fact, of another story in a similar genre.

Two rich men were neighbours. Each had a lovely wife and two children. Each had a beautiful house and several acres of land. Each had a good job in the city. Once a week the two couples met to play bridge. Their children went swimming together. Every summer the two families went to the South of France together. Mr Smythe and Mr Ffoulkes-Jones appeared to have an ideal friendship.

Mr Smythe had a yellow Rolls Royce which was his pride and joy. Mr Ffoulkes had a sleek, blue Jaguar which was his most dearly loved possession. The fact is that both men would have made less fuss if their wives had been unfaithful than if their cars had been damaged.

One day, unfortunately, the two men were involved in a minor motor crash. On the day of the accident they simultaneously drove out of their respective drives at precisely the same time as a motor cyclist went whizzing past at one hundred and twenty miles an hour. Each man had to take evasive action and the unhappy result was that they collided with sufficient force to make a nasty mess of one wing of each car.

Mr Smythe got out of his car and shouted, "Rodney, that a was a damned stupid thing to do!"

Almost at the same time Mr Ffoulkes-Jones got out of his car and yelled, "You bloody idiot Algernon!"

Each man got back into his car, slamming the door furiously. They both arrived at the local garage at the same time and, to the amazement of the garage owner, they both pulled away furiously and drove off in opposite directions.

A few days later, coincidentally on the same morning, each man received in the post an estimate for the cost of repairing the other's car, together with an invitation to send it to the insurance company. Rodney and Algernon then each marched across to the other's front door. They passed each other on the way and not speaking, posted back the estimates with curt notes saying that the accident was the other's fault. In fact, as it turned out, the insurance companies decided to split the costs. In the circumstances one would have thought that the two men would have then buried the hatchet. Unfortunately, such is human nature, that they continued to quarrel with some venom, their wives and children being forced to participate.

One day Mr Smythe lit a bonfire to get rid of some garden rubbish. A little smoke percolated into Mr Ffoulkes-Jones's house and he immediately ''phoned the police. On another day Mr Ffoulkes-Jones trimmed some trees and at the same time cut off some branches of one of Mr Smythe's overhanging shrubs. Mr Smythe instantly got his solicitor to write a threatening letter to Mr Ffoulkes-Jones.

Not unnaturally the two wives were fed up by this time and they started to have coffee in each other's houses while their husbands were at work. Likewise, the children went places together without the knowledge of their fathers, though with the connivance of their mothers.

One day I happened to call at the Smythe house to see if Mrs Smythe would support a charity for which I was secretary. Her name had been given to me by a member of the local congregation, though she herself was not a church person. When I called the two women were having coffee and I was invited to join them.

After I had been there for five minutes the two women looked at each other in a significant sort of way and I wondered if I had a smut on my nose or something. However, Mrs Smythe said, "I wonder if you can help us Brother Tristram."

"Yes, we'd be so grateful," said Mrs Ffoulkes-Jones.

I indicated that I would be happy to do anything within my power to help. Between them the two women related the story of the quarrel between their husbands. When they had finished I said, "What would you like me to do, ladies?"

"We wondered if you could give us any advice as to how to bring the quarrel to an end?" said Mrs Smythe.

"Or could you have a word with our husbands?" said Mrs Ffoulkes-Jones.

I don't usually pick up sticks of dynamite when the fuse is burning, so I said quickly, "It would be better if you two could resolve the problem. I'm sure I shouldn't interfere personally. However, if you want my advice I am willing to give it, for what it is worth."

They indicated that they would appreciate my advice. Now I have had a lot of experience of people's troubles and in that sort of situation I knew that what was required was that the two men should be placed in a position from which they could not escape and which at the same time would force them to speak to each other in a pleasant way. I also don't like to miss opportunities, so I decided to kill two birds with one stone, so I said, "I do have an inspiration. Suppose we invite both of your husbands to be present at the laying of the foundation stone of the new hospital wing that we're planning to build. That's what I came to see you about, actually. You could persuade each of them to donate a suitable sum and to make a speech, and then as they will be joint benefactors I will suggest that they shake hands before the assembled crowd. How does that sound?"

"Brilliant!" said Mrs Smythe.

"Amazing," said Mrs Ffoulkes-Jones.

I said modestly, "It was just an idea that happened to come to me. And then, of course, you two can invite some of the other benefactors to a dinner – probably on neutral territory. There's nothing like a glass of wine for making people convivial."

"You'll come, of course," said Mrs Smythe.

With some reluctance I agreed to attend the dinner. It's not that I don't enjoy a good cuisine, but my experience told me that the conversation would be mainly about business which I find rather boring.

The two men were, of course, astonished when they saw each other at the foundation stone ceremony. However, apart from a slight hiccup about which of them was to speak first, my scheme went like a dream. They smiled and shook hands as planned and the dinner invitations were given, apparently impromptu, by the two wives. However, when it came to the dinner, to my horror, the two men froze up and wouldn't speak to each other. I decided that an emergency action was required, so I said innocently, "I thought you two knew each other, as you are neighbours. Tell me, is there a well worn path between the two houses?"

I prayed that the two women would have the sense to remain quiet, which they did. Mr Smythe and Mr Ffoulkes-Jones spoke simultaneously and had to stop. Everybody laughed. Then they both said together, "After you." Everybody laughed again. From then on everything went well and the two men gradually became friends again.

The only thing is, about a year later I heard that Mr Smythe had run off with Mrs Ffoulkes-Jones. I realised, of course, that if I hadn't interfered such a thing might not have happened. Fortunately, or so some thought, Mr Ffoulkes-Jones consoled himself with Mrs Smythe.

Some time after that I heard that Mr Smythe and Mr Ffoulkes-Jones were very good friends, but that their new wives were not speaking to each other.

I am a great believer in the Golden Rule propounded long ago by Confucius. The rule suggests that a person shouldn't do to others what he would not wish others to do to him. I still believe it is a valuable piece of advice, but human nature is so perverse that it is difficult to put into practice. Moreover, events sometimes seem to have a mind of their own. Take the Smythes and the Ffoulkes-Jones's, for example, it is true that if all concerned had obeyed the Golden Rule, then presumably they would not have exchanged wives. However, it has to be remembered that it was a speeding motor cyclist who triggered off the chain of events that led to the outcome I have described, including my involvement in the affairs of the two families.

Actually, I have propounded a Golden Rule of my own. It is a simple one. I have resolved not to interfere in other people's affairs if I can avoid it. I suspect it is going to be a very difficult rule to keep.

23

The sphere of darkness

I once met a priest who had lost his faith in God. This is a terrible thing to happen to a priest, because he has gambled his whole life on an act of faith. Fr O'Connor, the priest in question, wanted a shoulder to cry on and I happened to be there.

When somebody wants to cry on my shoulder the first thing I always do is to offer him or her a cup of tea. It doesn't solve the problem, but it calms the nerves, especially mine. In these sorts of situations a man needs calm nerves.

So as we sipped our tea in my study Fr O'Connor said dismally, "I suppose I'll have to find another career."

I could see why he was dismal. It is not easy to start a new career when you are forty eight years old. I said, "Not necessarily. Suppose you find your faith again? Don't rush things."

"It's no good," he said. "I just don't believe God exists. How can I conscientiously preach the Gospel or celebrate mass if I don't believe in the things they stand for?"

"What made you think you were called to be a priest in the first place?" I said.

"Romanticism, I suppose. I thought I was destined to be a new Saint Paul who would go and build churches all over the world. Instead, I'm here in Acton and I'm completely lost."

"Even Saint Paul was shipwrecked," I said.

"I can do without your humour," he said tartly. "It's all right for you. You still believe in God."

"That wasn't always the case," I said.

"But you have since you became a priest."

"No," I said. "I had a crisis of faith about five years after my ordination. In fact, I felt exactly as you do now."

"How did you regain your faith, then?" he said hopefully.

I suppose it was a reasonable question in the circumstances. However, it wasn't an easy question to answer. I thought for a minute and then I said, "I pretended I had faith and then I found I really had it."

"That's a fat lot of help. In other words, you don't really have any faith at all."

"Of course I do," I said, "but you have to remember, as the good Book says, it is faith in things unseen."

"I know that," he said sarcastically, as if to imply that I was a complete idiot.

I said calmly, "You know all the arguments for God's existence put forward by Thomas Aquinas?"

"Of course," he said.

"You know the Christian creeds?"

"Do me a favour," he said.

"And you know the story of the Biblical revelation?"

"I'm not a child!"

"Are all those documents telling lies?" I said.

"Not lies as such, but the people who wrote those documents were deceiving themselves," he said.

"All of them?"

He thought for a moment and said, "Yes, the whole blasted lot of them. They've led us all up the garden path."

"Is that what faith is, to believe in those documents?" I said.

Again he thought. Then he said, "I suppose not. Faith in God is personal. But I've been over all these arguments. I'm not a complete fool."

"I know that," I said. "But if God is a person, would he deceive us through the documents we have been talking about?"

"By definition, if God exists, and it is an impossible if as far as I am concerned, I suppose you are right. God wouldn't tell a lie."

"All the people involved in writing those documents believed they were guided by God."

"So? I don't agree with them!"

"Let me ask you another question then," I said. "Were the witnesses to the resurrection telling the truth?"

"I don't believe they were telling lies. But they must have had a mass hallucination or something similar."

"Can you cross your heart and say you really believe that? I mean that they had hallucinations."

"I can't exactly cross my heart. But I can't accept that they really saw the risen Jesus. It's not logical. It does not fit in with our experience of death. They were the victims of wishful thinking. And that is what faith is, it's wishful thinking."

"So what am I doing when I say my prayers?"

Quick as a flash he said, "Whistling in the dark."

I was very tempted to say at that point, "Why don't we say a prayer together," but I decided against it. You see, I knew I had spotted a chink in his armour of faithlessness and if I asked him to pray with me I might lose my opportunity. Instead I sped a swift prayer to the Lord myself and said, "If the disciples were deceived in what they thought they saw, how do you explain the founding of the Church on the day of Pentecost? Was that a hallucination as well?"

I really had him there. He couldn't bring himself to say that there had been a further hallucination involving even more people. After a very long pause he said, "It was a long time ago."

I guessed that I had practically got him back on the rails, but I knew a further step was needed. I said, "I'll tell you what, why don't we try a bit of role reversal, just as an intellectual exercise?"

"How do you mean?" he said.

"I'll pretend I have lost my faith and you try to persuade me I'm wrong."

"You're trying to catch me out," he said.

"Very well," I said, "let me ask you some very searching questions instead."

"No. I don't wish to answer any more questions. Let's try this silly idea of yours."

I knew why he didn't want to answer any more questions. He was afraid of the answers. Anyway, I said breezily, "I don't believe in God. I can't see him or touch him, so he can't be there."

He said, "Have you really considered the alternative? It means living life hopelessly. What you are really doing is saying you have faith that there is no God. How can you have faith that there isn't a God? Can you prove it?"

"Yes," I said, thinking hard. There was a long pause while I racked my brains for a suitable answer. Finally I said, "If I explore the whole universe to infinity it will impossible to find God, so how can he be there?"

Fr O'Connor smiled mischievously and said, "That's impossible and you know it. Even if you could do what you say, you would only be proving that God cannot be shown to exist in space and time. That does not show he doesn't exist elsewhere."

"Where, for example?" I said sarcastically.

"In your mind, for a start. If you can imagine God at all, he must be in your mind. And then there is bound to be another dimension beyond this one. Surely you can see that. Logic demands it. This life as we know it is incomplete. It is developing. So where is it all going, tell me that?"

"To infinity," I said, "that's all there is to it."

"Do you mean to tell me that you accept infinity, one of God's characteristics. How about eternity? Do you believe in that as well?"

At that I burst out laughing and said, "You're back at the seminary again, aren't you?"

"So you give in?" he said triumphantly.

I gracefully but untruthfully admitted that I was defeated. He said, "My goodness, I feel better after that. There's nothing like a good argument to set the adrenalin going."

"Another cup of tea?" I asked innocently.

"Good heavens, look at the time. I must be off. I have to say mass in ten minutes. Thanks for the chat, Tristram."

And off he shot, bounding with energy. I knew he was over his crisis. I knew because it was true that I had been in his position. What that earlier experience taught me is that the mind has realms of related data. When we are living in a stable way these data are at the top of the mind and guide all our thoughts and actions. However, there are other spheres of the mind, the normally dark areas, and occasionally the mind moves into one of these spheres. The batches of related data that spring to mind may be from the past or they may be from things we have listened to or read. A good way to leap back to the normal sphere of the mind is to twist that sphere sharply into focus.

Quite often the mind then resumes its normal activities. If it doesn't then the dark sphere becomes the light sphere and the mind's set can be permanently changed.

I said a little prayer for Fr O'Connor and asked the Lord to let him stay in the sphere of light.

24

Fishing in Galway

I was on the ferry from Holyhead to Dublin once when I met a man who was going for a long weekend in his home county in Ireland. I happened to be telling my rosary while sitting comfortably in an armchair when this huge man came to sit beside me. When I had finished my rosary the man said, "Are you going somewhere special, Father?"

He spoke with a strong Irish accent and, as it was a Bank Holiday weekend in England, I guessed he worked in England but was going home for the weekend.

I said, "It depends what you mean by special. Are you going somewhere special?"

"To be sure I am," he said. "I'm going to Galway to do some fishing."

"That sounds attractive," I said. "I'm going to do some fishing myself, as a matter of fact."

"Sea or river?" he said.

"Neither," I said. "I'm fishing for men who might have vocations to the order I belong to. I'm visiting a seminary in Cork for that very purpose. It's like a holy careers convention if you like."

"It's no good looking in my direction, I'm a lapsed Catholic."

"I'm not sure what a lapsed Catholic is," I said. "Presumably you were baptized and had your first communion."

"Of course. But I no longer have anything to do with the church."

"Do you believe in God?" I said.

"Off and on."

I laughed. "I can see you're a comedian. What does off and on mean. Either God is there or he isn't."

"It depends where I am and what I'm doing," he said, smiling broadly. "When I'm fishing in Galway I definitely believe in God. When I'm working in the office I have very strong doubts."

"So you're really going to Galway to commune with the Lord?" I said.

He laughed. "It's you that's the comedian, Father. My name's Patrick, by the way."

"Brother Tristram," I said, shaking his hand.

We sat in silence for a while. Then Patrick said, "You're not Irish, Father?"

"No, I haven't that privilege. But I do have a lot of Irish friends. Ireland exports monks and nuns all over the world, you know."

"That won't do a lot for the balance of payments," Patrick said, grinning.

"It might do a lot for the balance of heaven and hell," I said.

"Don't they need converting in Ireland, then, Father?"

"They didn't used to. But I'm afraid that many Irish people are wearing the same shoes as you are."

"We were all brainwashed," he said sturdily. "You don't need to go to church to believe in God. The nuns didn't tell us that at school."

"Going to church every Sunday doesn't make you believe in God, but it does give you an opportunity to come to terms with yourself and life's problems. It gives people a bit of space and time to sort themselves out."

"I can do that when I'm fishing," he said.

"In other words, the act of fishing is really an act of worship," I countered.

"It's not the fishing itself," he said. "It's sitting under the sky and watching the scenery and listening to nature."

"I'm sure Jesus did that," I said.

"He also went fishing," said Patrick. "So you could say I'm following in the Lord's footsteps."

I must say I found Patrick very amusing. He was like a breath of fresh air filtering through to my ecclesiastical stuffiness. I said, "Perhaps all bishops should be compelled to do the same."

"Especially in Galway, Father. It would do them the power of heavenly good, to be sure."

I said, "Moses was right, you know."

"How do you mean?"

"When he said we all needed to take a day off for worshipping God. It stands to reason, doesn't it. If we went on day after day without stopping to take breath we'd all die at about the age of forty."

Patrick laughed. "I expect you're going to say that's why Moses lived till he was a hundred and twenty, Father."

I laughed as well. I was beginning to warm to this man. Then I said, "What do you do on Sundays in England, Patrick?"

"Go fishing, what do you think? At least when I have Sunday off," he said.

I resisted the temptation to suggest that he might try going to church occasionally. Instead I said, "Does that recharge your batteries?"

"It stops me from having a nervous breakdown," he said. "My job's not an easy one."

"May I ask what you do?" I said curiously.

"I'm the deputy governor of a prison."

That surprised me, I must say. I said, "I expect that has something to do with wanting to go fishing."

"To be sure, Father, it has everything to do with it. The trouble with church is it reminds me too much of prison. The Lord doesn't want us behind bars now, does he?"

"No," I said. "The Gospel is all about freedom. But I find going to church and the discipline of prayer sets me free. Setting apart time for God is a good way to be free from worry during the busy times."

"I don't disagree," he said. "But perhaps it's a matter of temperament. I get too much discipline. And I get too much friction. My answer to it all is to go fishing."

I was impressed by Patrick's line of reasoning. I said, "Tell me, Patrick, do you ever pray nowadays?"

"Not in the way you mean, Father, but I think about people and situations when I'm fishing and somehow I feel I'm commending all my problems and theirs to the Almighty. I suppose it's a kind of prayer."

"Some of my prayers are like that," I said. "I suppose the surroundings help the process. I like to be in chapel myself. The atmosphere just seems right somehow. But with you it seems to be communing with nature that helps the process."

"Yes," he said. "But I have a confession to make, Father. When I can't go fishing I sometimes go and sit in the prison chapel for a while. I find it helps."

Shortly after that we arrived in Dublin and I said goodbye to Patrick. I have never seen him since, but I do feel that my encounter with him taught me something important. I now know that people can find space and time for the Lord in different ways and who is to say what the Lord finds acceptable or not acceptable. One thing's for sure, I wish some of my colleagues would go fishing in Galway now and again.

25

The eighth deadly sin

I have noticed recently that my trousers are getting increasingly difficult to fasten. The reason for this will not be difficult for you to guess. Apart from Sister Ursula's sponge cake, I also enjoy the pleasures of a glass of wine now and again. No, I must be honest, "now and again" is not quite an accurate description. "More and more frequently" would perhaps fit the bill better. Anyway, I am eating and drinking far too much.

This led me to thinking philosophically about food in general and the aesthetic joys of an excellent cuisine. Then, by contrast, my thoughts turned to the traditional sin of gluttony. It is a parable about life I suppose. God has given us the wonderful gift of taste along with the necessity of eating to keep body and soul together. When the balance of these forces is right, then the result is supreme happiness. However, to eat either too much or too little may result in disastrous consequences. In my case, eating too much may result in the expensive purchase of a new wardrobe. It does not do a great deal for the comfort of my conscience when I see the results of eating too little in some Third World countries.

I once knew a man who lived for eating. Every available minute of every day was spent in anticipating the joys of eating, or in actually eating, or in enjoying the memory of the past pleasures of eating. It will not surprise you when I tell you that this man weighed over eighteen stones. He carried his weight well, however, and he was quite light on his feet. I know this because I was once present at a dinner dance where I observed him tripping easily on the light fantastic.

This habit of combining dining with dancing led to his downfall. A certain lady, for reasons best known to herself, took a shine for Friar Tuck, as he was jocularly called by his friends. As you know, it quite often happens that when a lady fancies a particular gentleman the result is a trip up the aisle. The day Friar Tuck tripped up the aisle, it was not on the light fantastic, I can tell you. He had had a bachelor party the night before which had resulted in a king sized hangover. The new Mrs Friar Tuck was not at all pleased. She put a brave face on things though, and smiled throughout the ceremony and the reception.

Actually, the names of the happy couple were Anthony and Enid. They both attended the church where I was working as a parish missioner. One day Enid came to see me and asked my advice. What she asked me should not surprise you. It was a classical case of the bride wishing to change the habits of the bridegroom. I should have observed the warning signs. However, while experience is a wonderful teacher I do not always learn my lessons well enough to know when it is wise not to interfere. In any case, not only am I a professional interferer, I was also born that way.

"How can I help?" I said affably when Enid came to see me.

"It's about Anthony," she said, smiling wistfully in a way that would melt a man's heart. By the by, Enid was not a slip of a girl. She was forty if she was a day, but a very well preserved forty. Her husband was slightly older.

I wondered what was coming next. In fact, I was dreading what might come next. However, when she said Anthony was eating far too much, I sighed with relief. That sounded a much safer subject to give advice on than many others I could think of.

"So why don't you persuade him to cut down a bit?" ¡ I said. "It needn't be too drastic."

116

"I'm frightened; he'll hate me if I make him eat salads instead of roast beef and Yorkshire pudding. He loves his food so much. But he doesn't know when to stop. After we've eaten the pudding he usually eats a piece of chocolate cake and two pears. And then between meals he likes to eat turkish delight, though sometimes he prefers coffee creams. It depends what mood he's in."

I wondered what kind of a mood you had to be in to prefer coffee creams to turkish delight. However, I said, "You'll have to be firm but kind."

"I don't think that's quite the right way," she said. "I wondered whether you would have a word with him, Brother Tristram?"

That sounded innocent enough. I said, "I suppose I could bring the subject up in a roundabout sort of way."

"I should be ever so grateful," she said, looking at me as if I were the only man in the world who mattered to her. She knew it was safe to do that, of course, because monks are "not to be touched." However, she also knew instinctively that I was a mere man like her husband and that I too had a soft spot for a petty female face.

"I know," I said, "I'll ask him to come round to discuss the churchyard. We're both on the churchyard committee and I do need some advice from an expert on gardening." Anthony was, in fact, a gardening enthusiast. I continued, "And when we've finished talking about gardening I'll gradually turn the subject round to the dangers of over eating."

And so it came about. Anthony and I chatted for about twenty minutes about the churchyard and then, as is my habit, I made us both a cup of tea. I refrained from opening my biscuit box, though I saw Anthony's eyes fixed upon it.

I asked Anthony how married life suited him and he said jokingly, "You should try it yourself, Brother Tristram, it would make a new man of you."

I said, "But is it going to make a new man of you,

Anthony? Don't you think you owe it to your wife to slim down a bit?"

"Do you really think so? I thought she liked me as I am."

"I'm sure she does," I said hastily, "but a man with your weight is surely risking a heart attack or something. Suppose you have a family. And then, God forbid, suppose you should be taken suddenly. What would happen to the little ones?"

Anthony's face became very serious as he contemplated his own early demise. The folds under his chin wrinkled as he lowered his head and stroked his chins.

"And then again," I said, "what about your immortal soul?"

"What about it?" he said anxiously, as if he felt his soul was in danger that very minute.

"I mean simply that if you die as a result of your own gluttony and thus cause unhappiness to your family, the case will be strong against you."

"What case?" he said, obviously concerned.

"I mean at the judgement seat," I said sternly.

His face fell and he placed his head between his hands. I had no idea he was so impressionable. If you threatened most people with the consequences of the sin of gluttony they would laugh and say, "It's a nice way to go."

"Do you really think so?" he muttered.

I decided to put the boot in. "I'm certain of it."

"Well," he said. "I've been a fool. My life has been resting on a knife edge and I had no idea. I just like eating, you see."

"So do I," I said, "but sometimes I think of other things like football or music. Why don't you try a simple diet, nothing too drastic?"

"You bet," he said, enthusiasm exuding from every inch of his corpulence. "I'll start right away."

The effects of Anthony's diet were remarkable. Within

a week you could see a distinct difference. Within a fortnight he had lost two and a half stones. Within a month he was a shadow of his former self. Unfortunately, after two months he was practically a skeleton. As my grandmother used to say, there's a difference between skinning a pig and slicing it into bacon.

Enid came along to see me. She was in tears. "It's all your fault," she sobbed. "You filled my poor Anthony's brain with your stupid ideas. He's dieting himself to death. I want my old Anthony back. He was so cuddly."

This was obviously a no win situation. I said, "I'll come and have a word with him."

"Today," she howled. "Now!"

What could I say? I went along with her. We found Anthony sitting in an arm chair, a glass of water in one hand and a water biscuit in the other. He looked almost senile, his face gaunt. I nodded to Enid to indicate that she should leave me alone with her husband. When she had gone I said gently, "Goodness me, what have you done to yourself, Anthony. I didn't intend that you should go this far."

"I'm winning, Brother Tristram," he said, smiling wanly. "I'm losing weight. I shall be a good father for the rest of my life."

The poor man looked as if the rest of his life could be a matter of a few days. I said, "Your wife is very upset, Anthony. You've gone much too far. She wants the man she married to come back again."

"What about the children?" he said.

"The way you're going you won't have the strength to produce any," I said. "You must eat."

"What about the sin of gluttony?" he moaned.

I could see I was going to have to eat my words. "Well," I said, "it is a sin of course, but it's an even greater sin not to eat at all."

He looked at me hopefully. "I haven't been at all happy.

119

The trouble is you see, I'm the sort of person who doesn't do things by halves."

There was only one thing for it. I said, "Forget about the sin of gluttony and eat what you like. When they defined the seven deadly sins they forget to mention the sin of starving yourself to death. That brings an even greater punishment than gluttony. You'll go to hell for all eternity."

I decided to leave him dramatically at that point. I said to Enid as I went out, "Make him something with chips. Steak, if possible. I think I've managed to change his mind."

It was amazing. Within three months Anthony was Friar Tuck again. He and his wife were deliriously happy. Twelve months later they had their first baby. He was a heavy weight like his father.

I pondered these events for a while and I came to the conclusion that some people can't take the middle road. They have to go to one extreme or the other. As for me, I'm an expert on the middle road, except in one matter. If Arsenal loses on a Saturday afternoon I'm in the dumps for a whole week. If they win I'm in heaven for a week. The football season is consequently something of a trial.

26

Behind the facade

In my line of business I meet a lot of people. To some extent people can be categorised, I suppose. For example, when you meet someone for the first time you can say, "Oh yes, he's a shy but kindly person," or, "She's a bossy boots." Yet, at the same time every person is unique. This means that first impressions often have to be modified. Let me explain what I mean.

I once met a man whom I immediately categorised as a first class swine to everybody he met, especially to those who worked for him. He was rude. He was inconsiderate. He was bad tempered. He had a twisted sense of humour which was usually expressed in sarcastic comments at other people's expense. His name was John Biggs, but behind his back everybody called him Big Mouth.

I met Mr Biggs when I was an industrial chaplain for a Midlands firm that made parts for aeroplane engines. The factory was not a large one, but it did quite well in its own specialist area. In addition to the workshops there were also playing fields and a staff club. It was generally reckoned to be a good firm to work for. Mr Biggs was the managing director and it was he who first interviewed me when I was appointed chaplain.

I can remember his red, angry looking face and fierce eyes as he said to me, "I think you're actually an excrescence, Brother Tristram. I don't agree with having chaplains in factories. Religion has nothing to do with what we do here. Still, I suppose you're another shoulder to cry on when somebody falls by the wayside. Some people have no bloody stamina, you know."

That was not a very auspicious start to a new job, even if it was only a part time position. I soon got to know people and I used to drop in mainly at lunch times. I saw my function as supportive, not only of people wearing their working hats, but also of people's personal lives outside the factory. Some of the workers never entered a church or a chapel, but I found the vast majority were good, God fearing people in their own simple way. Incidentally, I never wore my habit when visiting the factory because I felt it would frighten people off when they might want to have a heart to heart.

After I'd been visiting the factory for about three months Mr Biggs sent for me. When I entered his office his secretary hurried out, looking slightly embarrassed. When she had shut the door he barked, "Sit down!"

It was hardly an invitation to refuse. He then said, "I always knew the clergy were a bloody useless lot. Why haven't you done anything about Jack Williams?"

I said lamely, "I have no idea who Jack Williams is. Possibly I know him by sight...".

"Amazing," he said, "Absolutely amazing! Here is an opportunity for you to do something useful at last, and you don't even know who Jack Williams is."

"If you explain what the trouble is I might be able to do something about it," I said stiffly.

"The trouble is that the man has cancer and he's been given six months to live. Why haven't you visited his home? Goodness knows, the firm makes a large enough contribution to your church."

I said, "My job isn't easy, you know. I can only pick up problems from what people tell me."

"You clergy don't even know what work is," growled Mr Biggs. "You should try working on the factory floor for a while. Your eyes would be opened then, I can tell you. I started on the factory floor myself, so I know what I'm talking about."

A little bit of daylight dawned in my mind. Perhaps Mr Biggs was so inconsiderate and ill mannered because he wasn't sure of his position. Perhaps he was somebody who really needed reassurance and love. I wondered if he was married. I imagined that his wife might be a mousy little woman who was scared stiff of him. Actually, I was wrong about that. I met her later that year at the Christmas do. She was a big hearty woman and she said to me at the top of her voice, when I was introduced to her, "Don't let John boss you about. He's a big softie really."

I found this an amazing statement for anybody to make about Bossy Biggs, as I had come to call him in my own mind. However, I did see another side to his character when I visited Jack Williams. Naturally, I told Biggs that I would go to the Williams household right away. When I knocked on the door of the little terraced house, a thin and worn woman wearing a flower patterned apron opened the door. When I said who I was she invited me in and took me upstairs. Her husband was sitting up in bed reading. He closed his book when I entered the bedroom.

Jack Williams was paper thin and white faced. However, he smiled and said, "Nice to meet you, padre. I haven't been at work much since you arrived, but I've heard a lot about you."

I was slightly relieved to hear that he had been away from work a lot. It explained why I hadn't come across him. I chatted with Jack for half an hour or so. He was an easy man to talk to. Perhaps because, like me, he was a football enthusiast. After a while he said with a grin, "How are you getting on with Biggsie?"

I must have grimaced because Jack said, "Your face says it all. He's O.K. really. We started together as apprentices, you know. Believe it or not he was a quiet chap."

I said, "Why is he so rude and inconsiderate? Wouldn't he get more out of the work force if he treated them more like human beings?"

Jack laughed so heartily that it set him off coughing. It took him a couple of minutes to recover. Then he said, "Nobody's really frightened of him. His bark is worse than his bite. You ought to see him when he's really upset."

"I'd rather not," I said.

"You can take it from me that his heart's in the right place," insisted Jack. "Anyway you have to take people as you find them. When you've been with us a bit longer you'll see a different side to him. By the way, who told you about me?"

"As a matter of fact it was Mr Biggs," I said.

"There you are then. Wasn't that thoughtful of him?"

"He didn't exactly ask me very politely."

"Well he wouldn't, would he. It would spoil his image as the big bad wolf. He's putting it on most of the time you know."

We chatted on for a while. Then I could see that Jack was getting tired, so I made my excuses and left. I had a chat with Mrs Williams downstairs over a cup of tea. Before I left the house she said, "Mr Biggs has been ever so kind, you know. He's been round every week with fruit or flowers. And he talks to Jack for at least two hours every time he comes."

I was quite astonished by this revelation and I decided that I should have to revise my opinion of Bossy Biggs. However, though I watched him carefully, I never once saw him relax from his pose as the "big bad wolf". I came to the conclusion that he had only been kind to Jack Williams because of their time together as apprentices.

However, as I got to know more and more people at the factory I heard more and more stories about Mr Biggs and his kindly consideration for employees who were in difficulties. Eventually I had to admit to myself that Jack Williams had given a true assessment of Biggsie's character.

When I came to leave my post as chaplain because of

124

other duties, Bossy Biggs called me into his office. As usual he barked, "Sit down!"

I noticed that his secretary smiled affectionately behind his back as she left the room. He said, "I haven't changed my mind about chaplains, you know. I think they're a bloody nuisance. Still, if we had to have a chaplain I'm pleased it was you. I know you can't accept money personally, but I hope you will accept this cheque and see that it does some good for somebody. If ever you want a reference let me know."

With that he turned back to his work and ignored me. I thanked him and left, feeling more than a little confused. When I looked at the amount on the cheque he had given me I was astonished at the man's generosity.

People often say that beauty is skin deep and that what matters is the inner self. I suppose that must be true of all outward semblances and poses. True consideration for others lies at a much deeper level than is usually revealed to the world. Conversely, I have met people who present a polite and considerate face to the world, though internally they are filled with hate and jealousy. Of the two types I think I prefer Mr Biggs. On the other hand, it is possible to have the best of both worlds, the outer and the inner. Many people are genuinely considerate for others both on the surface and deep within their souls. They are the true salt of the earth.

27

The lazy angel

There was once an angel who became very lazy. This was an unhappy situation. I think you will agree, but when I tell you that he was a guardian angel I think you will conclude, as I did, that this was most unfortunate indeed for the human being who was being guarded.

The angel's name was Sopor. His besetting trouble was sleepiness while he was at work. Of course angels get very little rest, so it is not surprising if now and again one of them becomes sleepy. The chief angel called Sopor back to base one day and took him to task about his laziness.

The chief angel said sternly, "Look what a bad example you are setting for human beings. It's a deadly sin to be lazy and angels are supposed to be above that sort of thing."

"It's all very well for you to talk," said Sopor, "but when was the last time you did any guarding? As far as I can see you sit on your bottom all day gazing at that master of all computers."

"I'll change jobs with you any day," said the chief angel. "I could do your job standing on my head."

"Done!" said Sopor with a triumphant grin. He was well aware that telling lies was even more reprehensible than laziness and so he knew that the chief angel couldn't go back on what he had said.

Rather crestfallen the chief angel had to hand over the master of all computers to Sopor and then had to wing it down to earth to watch over Clarence Sopwith. Meanwhile Sopor was rubbing his hands because he knew that watching over Clarence Sopwith was the most boring job in all angeldom. That was why he had become so sleepy, thus acquiring a reputation for laziness. Or at any rate, that was his own theory.

The chief angel soon found that Clarence Sopwith very rarely did anything exciting. He was a bachelor with very fixed habits. He went to work on the underground at precisely the same time each morning. He returned home at precisely the same time each evening. His brief case always contained the same sort of sandwiches together with a flask of milkless and sugarless tea. He always had either poached egg or baked beans for the evening meal. He watched television for three hours every evening and then went to bed straight after the evening news. Oh, and I forgot to say, he always failed to complete the crossword on his way to work.

The chief angel had a very positive outlook. That was why he was the chief angel. He decided to make Clarence's life more exciting. He had seen at a glance that his new ward was a very worthy man. He pondered for a day or two as to the best way to give Clarence's life a bit of zip. Finally, he decided that what Clarence needed was a wife. "That should give him some excitement," thought the chief angel, "especially if he becomes a father."

The chief angel scouted round for a suitable woman. While he was following Clarence to work each morning he noticed that a not unattractive lady about ten years younger than Clarence always travelled on the same train to work. She knitted socks all the way there and, indeed, all the way back. "Goodness me," said the chief angel to himself, "she needs some excitement too. Perhaps if I can bring the two together it will cause a cosmic explosion of love."

That was expecting a lot, I suppose, but nevertheless the chief angel's tactics soon began to work. He arranged for the lady, whose name was Letitia, to drop her knitting just as Clarence was passing. She blushed furiously, but Clarence perceived this pink suffusion of her face as a compliment to himself and sat down beside Letitia. Friendship blossomed into romance. Romance blossomed into marriage. And, to the chief angel's delight, the marriage bore fruit.

Now I hardly like to suggest that the thought of watching over Clarence's sleepless nights caused the chief angel to think it was time he went back to base, but that is certainly what he decided to do. Of course, he was also slightly concerned about the state of his master of all computers which had been entirely in the hands of Sopor. However, the computer was working efficiently and the print outs of angel responsibilities were in good order.

The chief angel concluded that a change of occupation had cured Sopor of his laziness. When he thought about this further he decided to issue a directive to all guardian angels on how to deal with the sin of laziness in human beings. This is what he wrote:

"As we all know laziness is one of the most deadly of all the sins because it leads to inefficiency. Windows do not get cleaned. Gardens do not get weeded. People become fat. A lot of unhappinesss is caused to others. Laziness also leads to lack of purpose in life. We have long sought a cure for this sin and while a complete and lasting cure may not be found, there is one way of alleviating the condition. Ensure that your ward does not become a creature of habit. Try to find him another job, one that will bring new interests into his life."

Meanwhile, Sopor went back to his post of guarding Clarence. When he eventually received the directive from the chief angel he was furious. Since his return he had never had an hour's peace. Clarence's life was all upside down. Not only was he constantly walking around at night rocking the new baby, he was also incredibly cheerful. One morning he even succeeded in completing the crossword, much to the exasperation of all the nearby commuters who had never managed to complete it. Clarence also became a bundle of energy at work and received a promotion. It was all about having the right motives, I suppose. Now that he had three mouths to feed, instead of one, he felt he had to put his best foot forward.

When Sopor thought about this he sent a fax to the chief angel saying, "Thank you for your directive about laziness. My experience is that it is not a new job in itself which shakes people up so much as extra responsibilities. Why do we not try to make lazy people more responsible for the welfare of other people?"

The chief angel was a fair minded person and he could see that this message was relevant to all the guardian angels, so he sent out a further directive incorporating Sopor's principle that responsibility cures laziness. After all, it was responsibility that had cured Sopor, not just the new job. You see, the master of all computers controls the affairs of all angels and all human beings. Any old job wouldn't have cured Sopor. It was the weight of responsibility that did the trick.

28

A glimpse of beauty

Sister Ursula and I were talking about beauty the other day. Not that either of us could be described as beautiful. What started us off was the idea that any human being could be described as ugly, which is a different matter altogether. Sister Ursula said that she didn't mind not being a beauty, but she was glad that she wasn't ugly. I took her up on that point right away by saying, "But sister, every human being is created by God. To him we must all be beautiful."

"Rubbish!" she said. "It's obvious that we aren't all equally beautiful. Take you for example. Are you telling me that God regards you as beautiful?"

Put like that I suppose it did sound a bit unlikely. However, I stuck to my point and said, "You have a wonderful way of missing the point, Sister. Every human body is a miracle of precision engineering. The features on the face are functional as well as beautiful and the shape of one person's nose compared with another's is immaterial."

She thought for a moment and then she said, "It's the relationship between the features that makes a face beautiful. Take Marilyn Munro, for instance. You can't surely say that her nose is of the same standard of beauty as yours. I'm not saying there's anything wrong with your nose, of course, but you lost the argument when you said it was functional."

"What about the beauty of the soul?" I said, sliding off the subject of my nose.

"If there is such a thing," she said ironically, "it's quite obvious that some souls must be more beautiful than others."

I decided it would be wise not to continue the discussion, but on the way home I pondered the question of beauty and how important it is in human life. I remembered how I once met a child who had very little appreciation of beautiful things. It wasn't surprising, because the child in question lived in an East End street and rarely saw either the sun or the stars, much less one of the city's public parks. The kind of programmes she watched on television were not exactly inspiring. In any case, the child, whose name was Rebecca, spent her time trying to earn a little money for her widowed mother and the rest of the family. As often as not she wasn't at school. Rebecca was the oldest child in the family and I guessed it wouldn't be long before she was forced by circumstances into prostitution. I had seen it happen before.

It's very difficult for a monk to befriend a fourteen year old girl. His motives can so easily be misunderstood. But I did wish that something could be done to expand her horizons. It may seem a bit unfair to try to help just one girl when so many other boys and girls were in the same boat. However, one of my principles has always been that when you are surrounded by chaos you have to start somewhere in the attempt to clear it up. So I said a prayer and asked Sister Ursula, who was a lot younger then, if she could help.

We decided between us that what Rebecca needed was a trip to the country, not just for an afternoon, but for a weekend. The girl had never been out of London before. Sister Ursula had an old school friend who ran a country hotel near Winchester. Ursula was invited to stay there now and again. Normally she didn't angle for invitations, but on this occasion she specifically asked if she could spend a weekend at the hotel and bring a friend. The permission of Rebecca's mother was obtained and the girl herself agreed to go, though her pale face and listless manner showed no excitement at the prospect of a weekend away.

Of course, I had to wait at home wondering how the weekend was going. Naturally I was hoping that Rebecca would receive some kind of revelation that would open her eyes to the richness of the created world.

Sister Ursula duly delivered Rebecca home on the Sunday evening. I happened to see Sister Ursula arriving at the convent so I hurried over, eager to find out what had happened. As usual Sister Ursula insisted on pouring me a cup of tea before she would utter a word on the topic I was so interested in. She can be exasperating sometimes. However, at last she said, "I suppose you want to know how Rebecca enjoyed herself?"

"Yes. Did she have a good time?"

"I somehow don't think the weekend made much impact on her."

"But surely, Sister, you showed her all sorts of exciting things."

"Of course I did, you silly man. Do you think I'm a fool?"

I valued Sister Ursula's Victoria's sponge cake too much to make any comment, facetious or otherwise.

She went on, "I showed her the cows being milked. I took her into the woods and we found sixteen different kinds of wild flowers. We went to feed the swans and ducks on the river. Goodness me, we did all sorts of things. But for the whole weekend the girl never smiled once. When I asked her how she enjoyed it she just said, 'It was all right, I suppose.'"

"Didn't you take her down to the sea?"

Sister Ursula gave me a withering look. "Of course I did. We even went paddling."

At that time I could well have imagined Sister Ursula paddling, though it would stretch the imagination a bit nowadays. Anyway, I said, "So the weekend was a failure?"

"I wouldn't say that," she said. "Just occasionally I

perceived a gleam in the girl's eyes as if she had caught sight of heaven for an instant."

I had to make do with that at that time. There was, however, a sequel. Rebecca began to attend school more regularly and the art teacher, who knew I was concerned about the girl, said to me one day, "Rebecca seems to have found a previously hidden talent. You ought to see some of the pictures she's doing."

"What sort of thing is she producing?" I asked curiously.

"She's painted a masterpiece of a swan. And she did a flowery wall paper pattern that the Queen wouldn't be ashamed to have in her bedroom."

As soon as I got the opportunity I went over to tell Sister Ursula of this wonderful news. Her reaction was a little muted. "Perhaps it's a flash in the pan," she said.

I'm more of an optimist myself. I said, "I'd like to see her go to art school. I'm sure she's a budding artist."

I'm not often proved right when it comes to differing from Sister Ursula, but in this case I was proved right. The girl did go to art school and she is now a lithographic artist and doing very nicely thank you.

I must remember to remind Sister Ursula about Rebecca next time we get onto the subject of beauty.

My own thoughts went a little bit further. It struck me that a few snatched glimpses of beauty had changed a girl's life. What would happen if all the schools began to teach beauty as the main item on the curriculum. I'm not suggesting, of course, that children should give up maths or science. Indeed, those subjects contain their own revelations of beauty. But just suppose the appreciation of beauty was given a high priority in all schools. The results might be amazing. I must try my theory out on Sister Ursula next time I see her.

29

How to charm the green-eyed monster

Even if Cain and Abel were not real characters, as some people say, their behaviour in the Bible story was certainly typical of the human species. The writer of that story must have observed the disastrous effects of envy. It can be very destructive of both the envious and the object of envy. If you remember, Abel lost his life because his envious brother murdered him, while Cain, the murderer, was condemned to wander the face of the earth. In other words, nobody wins in that kind of situation. I am reminded, in fact, of a similar story. I once knew somebody who was as venomous as Cain because of the envy which consumed him.

Two men were very great friends. They had known each other since they were toddlers. They had gone to the same sequence of schools. They had joined the army together. They had gone to the same university. They had both married well and both had good jobs. Indeed, they had both done equally well up to the point where my story begins.

In one respect, however, they differed. Each man belonged to a different political party. This was not for many years a cause for dissension. Rather it led to a lot of leg pulling on either side. It was not until both men were invited to stand for Parliament that the trouble started. It would have been less divisive if they had stood in different constituencies. In fact, they both stood for the same Parliamentary seat and, moreover, there were no other candidates. In other words, one was bound to win and one was bound to lose.

The contest began amicably enough. Indeed, they shook

hands and undertook to fight fairly and to accept the result without rancour whatever it might be. However, it was decided that during the campaign they had better go their separate ways.

Jeremy was a staunch member of the Monarchy party which was very traditional in its approach. Trevor belonged to the Christian Democratic party which was very radical in its policies. The names of the parties were a little misleading. The Monarchists had little to do with the monarchy. The name had become attached to the group hundreds of years previously and nobody had ever bothered to change it. The Christian Democrats had little to do with the Church, though the roots of the party had been developed originally within Church circles. Anyone could be a member of the Monarchical party without necessarily supporting the monarchy and likewise anyone could join the Christian Democrats without being a Church member.

It will not surprise you to know that the hot issues of the day were taxes and education. Put simply, the Monarchists wanted to lower taxes and to put less money into the education system, arguing that parents should contribute directly to schools. The Christian Democrats, on the other hand, wanted put more money into the education system and this would mean higher taxes for everybody.

In the town of Meldrum on the Weald, where Jeremy and Trevor were opposing each other, the arguments were more or less on party lines on these two issues. However, a certain spanner thrower decided to change the situation and wrote an open letter in the local press to each of the candidates. In this letter he challenged the two men to hold a public debate in the local town hall.

Both candidates agreed to this suggestion and on the evening in question the town hall chamber was full to capacity. At first the questions were about taxes and education and fairly stock answers were given. Then the spanner thrower acted decisively, according to a predetermined strategy. Everyone knew it was he who had suggested the debate, so the chairman readily gave him the opportunity to ask a question of the two beaming candidates.

The question the spanner thrower asked was, "What are the candidates' views on the new bypass which is to go through Togwell Forest?"

This particular issue had raised a lot of people's blood pressures locally, but it had not been in any sense a national issue. There had not even been any mention of the bypass in the national press. Jeremy was foolish enough to answer the question first. He said, "It stands to reason that this must be a good thing for this town. The traffic will pass along the new road and nobody will then come to our town to fill the High Street with traffic."

There were catcalls and boos at this statement. Many of the people present were shopkeepers and they wanted people to continue to come right through the middle of the town. They were worried in case they should lose business. In fact, the spanner thrower himself was a business man and he wanted to publicise the opposition to the bypass for his own selfish reasons.

Of course, Trevor could see which way the land lay before he gave his response. He said, with a very wise expression on his face, "Of course, I am dead against the bypass, as anyone with any sense must be. It would be a great loss to the town if traffic ceased to pass through the High Street. People would never see the amenities we have to offer here, not to mention the examples of beautiful architecture."

There was a rousing cheer when he sat down. Trevor smiled triumphantly at Jeremy, but the latter sat with a very sulky expression on his face.

The issue of the bypass was sufficient to swing the election Trevor's way. He won an easy victory. Jeremy was so upset that on the night after the election he went on a pub crawl round several neighbouring villages. He was alone and he was driving. On the way home he was stopped by a policeman. Jeremy refused to blow into the breathalyser and swore at the policeman. The policeman remonstrated with him. Jeremy then punched the policeman on the nose. Without further ado the policeman clapped the cuffs onto Jeremy's wrists and took him to the station where he was charged with assault and with driving while under the influence.

The following day Jeremy was in his car again, having been given bail. By some mischance Trevor happened to be crossing the road just as Jeremy was driving up. All of Jeremy's envy and frustration suddenly came to a head and he drove straight at his erstwhile friend.

The end result of this further assault was that Trevor was so badly injured that he became an invalid for the rest of his life. Jeremy was found guilty of malicious assault and spent fifteen years in gaol. And the two men never spoke to each other again.

I came to the conclusion after this episode that envy can rise within a person as suddenly as a volcano erupts and that it can be almost as dangerous. The only answer, if you are ever consumed by this emotion, is to wave it away humorously. Laugh at yourself and your ridiculous envy and the sting will be removed. Humour is one of the most creative emotions human beings can experience. It is also a great healer. However, do not let your humour turn into a vicious parodying of the object of your envy. Your humour would then surely turn round and bite painfully into your own soul. In any case, to decry your neighbour is to deny God's love.

30

Fighting a losing battle

I once had a very sharp argument with Sister Ursula. She maintained that for a Buddhist to bow to the statue of a Buddha was an infringement of the first commandment. Naturally I pointed out that the Ten Commandments are really a Jewish document and that it would be unfair to judge Buddhists by the standards of another faith. When I made that comment I saw that steely glint in her eye which usually indicated that I had strayed into the holy ground of one of her immovable principles. Being foolhardy by nature I decided to try to change Sister Ursula's opinion. So I said, "Anyway, Buddhists don't believe that Buddha is a god."

She said sharply, "A statue is a statue and if you bow down to it you are worshipping another god. The Ten Commandments were revealed by God to Moses and Christians have rightly adopted them. It is wrong to worship other gods whether you're a Buddhist or a Trappist."

I laughed, "I can hardly imagine a Trappist breaking the first commandment."

She was infuriated by my amusement. She said, "Trappists have been known to imitate eastern methods of meditation. In my view that is dangerously near breaking the first commandment. They chant meaningless words like OM for hours on end. What's that but a way of worshipping some peculiar other god?"

"You chant your rosary endlessly," I argued. "Aren't you making Our Lady into a sort of god?"

"Claptrap! Our Lady was and is the Mother of God.

Every child knows that. The Mother of God can't be God."

The logic of that seemed unanswerable, but I still thought she had completely missed the point. I said, "Buddhists don't believe in a personal God anyway. Not in the way we do."

"That makes it even more dangerous," she snapped. "They're going through the motions of worship in front of the statue of a man. In other words they make a man into a god."

"Buddhists have almost the same rules as we do," I said. "It's a highly ethical religion. No stealing, no adultery, no coveting, no killing. And that applies even to insects. It's a very bad thing to kill a cockroach."

I don't know why I mentioned "cockroaches". Spiders would have done just as well. But women have an inbuilt hatred of cockroaches and so Sister Ursula's reaction was inevitable and swift. She said decisively, "Any religion which says you mustn't kill cockroaches is evil."

I knew absolutely that nothing would ever unconvince her of that. If I wanted to win the argument I would have to change my ground. I thought for a moment and then said, "Take nature worship. Suppose a tribe hasn't heard of the Gospel. What alternative have they got? They look around the world and they see marvellous powers in nature. It seems natural to make them into gods. Our God isn't going to condemn them for their ignorance, is he?"

"If such tribes exist," she said, "Why aren't you out there telling them about the Gospel?"

As you can see, Sister Ursula is very skilled at not answering a question in such a way that it looks as if she has answered it. As I was familiar with this tactic of hers I said quickly, "Suppose they are completely isolated on a small planet way out in the solar system. Nobody is ever going to reach them with the Gospel. Is God going to condemn them?"

She said, "They'll hear the Gospel when they die. If they believe it they will be forgiven."

I decided to shift my ground again. I felt very much as if I were fighting a losing battle. However, I was determined not to give up. I said, "Most of the higher religions believe in a Supreme Being and they recommend similar codes of conduct. So the Christian God must be the same God as the God other religions believe in."

Sister Ursula thought for a moment. Then she said, "I can think of three reasons why other religions don't believe in the same God as Christians do."

She paused as if to give me an opportunity to jump in with both feet. However, I decided it would be wiser to hear her reasons first, so I waited for her to go on. She continued, "First of all no other religion believes Jesus is God's Son. Secondly, they don't believe in the Trinity. Thirdly, they don't accept God's true revelation."

"But if they believe in a Supreme Being," I countered, "they must believe in the same God as we do. There is after all, only one Supreme Being."

"Quite illogical," she said calmly. "If they define God in a different way they must be talking about a different god."

"You are missing my point, Sister," I said doggedly. "Even if they are slightly mistaken in their definition of God, as there is only one God they must be worshipping the same God."

"You are trying to excuse an error," she said. "It won't do, Brother. An error is an error, whichever way you look at it."

I didn't dare say that Christians might be the ones in error. After all an argument is only an argument and the loss of companionship over cups of tea and chocolate biscuits would be almost the loss of a way of life. It wasn't worth the risk. Instead I said, "You are the one who is in error, if you will excuse me for saying so, Sister. God loves everyone and he is the God of all nations. It says so in the

Bible. Therefore other people who worship God, even if it is in a different way, even if it is under a different definition of God, must be acceptable to God."

That was when she really floored me. Quite coolly she said, "Dear Brother, the argument is about breaking the first commandment. What you are saying is irrevelant. If everybody believes in the same God then nobody is breaking the first commandment."

I felt as if my king were in check. I recovered quickly and said, "So you agree that the higher religions all worship the same God?"

She shot back, quick as a flash, "That's what you said, not I. You must really learn not to turn your arguments inside out."

I was completely lost by that time. After a long pause which she refused to interrupt I said, "I'll grant you one thing. If somebody consciously worships another god then he or she must be breaking the first commandment."

"Leave the female sex out of it," she said. "Women are far too sensible to break the first commandment. Anyway they have other things on their minds, like looking after all the lazy men in the world. However, as you have conceded the argument I shall offer you another cup of tea."

Now it hadn't been my intention to concede the argument. I had merely been putting forward another pawn. However, the thought of another cup of tea was an attractive one, so I accepted gracefully and said, "By the way, the girls in the school put on a great Carol Service the other day."

31

The illuminated scroll

Whenever my sister bought a pair of shoes which were slightly too small for her, my mother used to say, "Pride's painful." My mother is now long gone and I suppose my sister buys more sensible shoes today, though I can't guarantee that such is the case. However, I had cause to think of that saying of my mother's recently.

One of the brothers in our monastery had always been a perfectionist. As a matter of fact, it was a policy of the brotherhood to aim for perfection in all we undertook, so it can hardly be said that Brother Ambrose was being sinful when he insisted that everything should be perfect. Certainly he put the rest of us to shame. His room was never untidy. He was never late for chapel. He never lost his temper. He never swore. I expect he never had lascivious thoughts, though of course only he knew whether he had or not. In other words, as far as the rest of us could see, his daily life was as ordered as creation before Adam and Eve nibbled the apple.

Brother Ambrose's main occupation was to paint illuminated scrolls. This activity may seem a little out of date for a modern monk, but actually, hand produced illuminated scrolls are in great demand. People like aldermen and honorary doctors prefer the hand produced variety to the machine made ones. It stands to reason, doesn't it? If a man or woman is being honoured for a cause, then the honour needs to be commemorated in a historical way – and you can't get more historical than an illuminated scroll.

I can tell you truthfully that Brother Ambrose's scrolls

were a marvel and a wonder of perfection. His capitals were decorated with exquisite animals and flowers. His ordinary letters were of the exact shape and size required. He never made a spelling mistake. Nor did he commit any of the other seven deadly sins of the scribe such as haplography or dittography. Occasionally I used to watch him working. Naturally I hardly dared breathe on these occasions. But I can honestly say it made me proud in a good sort of way to belong to the same order as a man who could produce such perfect specimens of illumination. I often think that Brother Ambrose should have been a monk in mediaeval times. If he had been, I am certain that some examples of his work would now be sitting in glass cases in the British Museum or in Trinity College, Dublin. As it is, his work is now decorating the studies of many worthy people.

One day an illuminated scroll that Brother Ambrose had produced was returned by a university. I shall be kind and not name the university in question. There was a note attached to the returned scroll which read, "Sorry, this scroll is not of a high enough standard. We wish to cancel our order."

Well, not only did Brother Ambrose nearly have a nervous breakdown, but the whole monastery was buzzing with horror. How could anyone say that one of Brother Ambrose's scrolls was not of a high enough standard? The scroll in question was put on display in our monastery library. Every monk examined it carefully, but couldn't find any fault with it. All the sisters from the convent came to look and none of them could find any fault with it either. Even Sister Ursula insisted that the scroll was a masterpiece and as perfect as human hands could make it.

It so happened that I had an old friend who was on the staff of the university concerned. We had studied in seminary together. He had been a high flier, while I had been a low swooper. Hence our careers had been very different.

Nevertheless we still corresponded and had a meal together from time to time. By a strange coincidence Fr Gerard was a member of the faculty which was about to confer an honorary doctorate upon a well known theologian. I wrote to Gerard and said I was going to be near the university. By return of post came an invitation to spend an evening in College with him. I indicated that I should be delighted.

After dinner, while Gerard and I were having coffee in the lounge, I said casually, "I hear Père Francois Milieu is receiving a D.D. from the Faculty of Theology."

"Good heavens!" he said, "How on earth did you hear that? It was all hushed up."

"How do you mean?" I said curiously.

"Well, naturally it was assumed that Milieu would be delighted to receive a doctorate from us. After all, he was a post graduate student here twenty five years ago. It was all planned. Even the scroll was got ready, I believe. And then Milieu turned down the offer."

"My word!" I said. "That's incredible."

"It is, isn't it. But the fact is that discreet enquiries turned up what we think was the true reason for his refusal. Mind you, we can't be certain, but I'm sure myself it is so."

"Do go on," I said, as he paused and sipped his coffee.

"Well, the Dean was here at the same time as Milieu. They were both researching in the same area. The Prof at the time, Biedenbacker, you know, mentioned the present Dean's research in an important book, but Milieu received no mention at all. Apparently the wound has festered all these years, and even though Milieu is arguably more eminent than the Dean, he still resents the insult he believes he received."

"Was he justified?" I asked, wanting the full story to retail to my brothers.

"Not really. Biedenbacker would have had to alter his book quite a lot to include Milieu's findings. Anyway, the

Dean was very miffed and insisted that the offer should never be made public. How on earth did you hear about it?"

On some occasions tact seems to overcome absolute honesty, so I said, "A friend happened to mention it."

This, of course, was not untrue. I then said, "I expect the scroll would be worth a bit in times to come. Rather like a postage stamp with a misprint on it."

"It's funny you should say that," said Gerard. "I happen to know that the Dean sent the scroll back to the artist saying it wasn't quite right, or something. It was thought better not to let even the artist know that the university had received such an insult. It was already paid for, I understand, so I don't suppose the artist would be bothered."

"He would be bothered if he was a perfectionist," I said.

"My dear chap, you weren't the artist, were you?"

"No. No. Not my line at all. But what a fascinating story."

"You won't spread it abroad, will you?" he said.

"Of course not," I said, with my fingers crossed behind my back.

Though I felt it would be right to tell the brothers, would swear them to secrecy, thus keeping the essence of my promise. After all, justice demanded that Brother Ambrose should be vindicated in his own community.

When I returned to the monastery I asked the Prior if I could tell the story at our next chapter meeting. He readily agreed. When I had finished my tale, Brother Ambrose was beaming. The Prior said, "Perhaps in a hundred years time the scroll could be valuable. Let's put it in a safe place for posterity."

The Prior was not the man to miss such an opportunity.

A few days after my revelation, Sister Ursula said to me, "Brother Ambrose seems to have got over his loss of face very well."

I was very tempted to tell her the story, but decided

against it. It wouldn't have been in the spirit of my promise to Fr Gerard. I said, "Pride is very painful for some people. My mother often used to say so. Perhaps Brother Gerard has overcome that particular human failing. He is a perfectionist, you know."

She looked at me in disbelief, but did not pursue the matter. Instead she said, "Another piece of chocolate cake?"

Now that is a human weakness. Chocolate cake, I mean. And I have not yet overcome it. But then, I'm not a perfectionist.

32

Brother Tristram beats the law

I'm not normally the sort of person who takes part in public demonstrations. Nor am I the sort of person who seeks notoriety. However, my conscience is a prickly one and on account of it I was once placed in a position where I had to make a public spectacle of myself in both of these ways. It is easy to say, "Well, you brought it upon yourself." No doubt this is true, but now and again the Lord demands that we stand up and be counted.

I was in a foreign country at the time. The whole area was troubled by civil war, workers' strikes, corruption in high places and general disorder. However, the judiciary of this particular country had always had a high reputation for fairness and integrity. This was the one bright star in the darkness of stormy times.

A certain wealthy man owned a large estate there. Part of this estate was a village which had stood for over a hundred years. The people were poor, though each family held a lease on a small piece of land which they farmed assidu-ously. The men in each family also had part time jobs to help them to eke out a precarious existence. The man who owned the estate, Baron von Stunkenbaum, also owned the prop-erty which had been leased to the families of the poor farmers until the year 2099. However, the Baron wanted to buy back the leases, including the one on the village church where I happened to be the temporary priest. He wanted the land to build a mansion for his eldest son who was about to be married. He and his son had set their hearts on this plan because that part of the estate was so beautiful.

Some of the villagers came to ask my advice. They had been offered substantial sums of money to surrender their leases, but they did not wish to leave their village for the same reason as the son of the Baron wished to take it over. The villagers had become very attached to their idyllic surroundings and wished to spend the rest of their lives there. As far as the church was concerned, the Baron had also made a generous offer. He pointed out that if the village was no longer there, then the church would be redundant. The local Bishop had taken the view that he would let events take their course. If the village was to be phased out of existence, then the Church would accept the offer. If, however, the village remained, then the church would remain. That left me in the driving seat. It's amazing how often bishops manage to leave their clergy holding the leaking baby, as they used to say in that country.

The advice I gave was simple. I told the villagers that if they wished to stay where they were they had the law on their side. On the other hand, if they wished to start a new life with a reasonable sum of money they had the opportunity to do so. In other words, I didn't decide for them. I merely explained the options. As it turned out every single villager decided to stay.

Baron von Stunkenbaum was furious. He blamed me for the obstinacy of the villagers. He swore he'd change his will so that the Church didn't receive a penny of his fortune. My reaction to that was to say that his money would come to God one day anyway, as all things did. The Baron actually knocked on my door one morning and talked to me for thirty five minutes about persuading the villagers to see semse. I could only reply that it was up to each lease holder to make up his own mind. Nevertheless, I undertook to have another chat with all the leaseholders. A meeting was called. I announced that the Baron had doubled the amount of money he was offering to each family for the surrender of their leases. I explained once again the details of what would be involved. In the event, not one villager was willing to sell his lease. That was when the Baron began to fight dirty.

What he decided to do was build a very tall fence on his own property, but in such a way that the marvellous views to which the villagers were accustomed were blocked. When I say a tall fence, I mean one of twenty feet. The Baron circled the village with his fence, carefully leaving rights of way for the villagers on the two roads that led out of the village. The only way you could see over the fence was to climb to the top of the church tower. It was like living in a prison camp.

I went with two villagers to the nearby town to take legal advice. The very expensive lawyer told us that the baron was within his rights. A man could build what he liked on his own property. There were no environmental planning laws in the country. I asked if there was a law about blocking the view from somebody's window. I think in England it's called the right of ancient lights, or something similar. The lawyer explained that the immediate views from the windows of the houses were not blocked. The law merely said that you couldn't build a fence within ten feet of your neighbour's windows.

Still the villagers stuck to their guns. One person suggested putting the houses on stilts, but it was agreed that this really wasn't practical. The Baron tried another ruse. He owned two very noisy helicopters. He started flying these low over the village at all hours of the day or night. It must have cost him a fortune in fuel, but then he had a thousand fortunes.

Off we went back to town to see the lawyer. He explained that you couldn't trespass in an aircraft unless you actually landed and in any case, the Baron ultimately owned the village, even though the property was leased out. When I asked about the laws of nuisance he shrugged his shoulders and said there were no such laws. I was beginning to see why the judges in that country had such a high reputation for justice. It was probably because they had so few laws, which made the job an easy one.

Still the villagers held out. The Baron then thought of another dirty trick. He blocked the stream which ran through the village. It was true that there was a well, but it was very inconvenient to draw every drop of water you needed from the village well and the women were no longer able to do their laundry in the running water of the stream.

The villagers called a meeting to which I was invited. It was decided that they could not afford another piece of advice from the lawyer. As in most countries, legal advice can be outrageously expensive. Once again they asked my advice. I said, "The only way to stop the Baron is through the courts. I believe justice is on your side, but following the law is not always equivalent to justice."

One elderly man said, "Let's sue the Baron. We'll fight him in the courts. He is spoiling the quality of our lives deliberately. Surely there must be a law against such actions."

Another man shouted, "We can't afford a lawyer!"

The first man said, "Brother Tristram will be our lawyer. We shall have a demonstration at the town hall to publicise our case."

Some people have greatness thrust upon them and it looked as if my hour had come. I was not looking forward to it, I can tell you. They hadn't taught us in the seminary how to fight legal battles. I would have to rely upon my native wit and the Lord's guidance.

When our case came to court the very lawyer who had been advising us was acting for the Baron. This was distinctly galling. Moreover, while he had been advising us he had been kind and gentle, but now he took on the appearance of a monster and behaved like one.

In brief, the lawyer argued that the Baron was acting within his legal rights. He had not interfered directly with the property leased by the villagers. The fence was there to block his own view of a very undesirable part of his estate. The helicopters were flying to spray crops and it was only occasionally they had to pass over the village. If they didn't do that they would have to waste fuel by flying great circles to go round it. The stream had been blocked because it was drastically altering the landscape which the Baron so admired.

The three judges were inscrutable during this tangled web of deceitful statements. For my part I based our case on two grounds. One was on the basis of commonsense. I could see the judges were not too impressed by that argument. My other argument was based on the natural justice which God had built into his universe. I was extremely careful not to criticise the legal system in any way. The main tenor of my argument was that the villagers had leased the property when it had good views and before helicopters were invented. They also had fishing rights in the stream as part of the original agreement and that right had now been taken away. Mind you, I was on very tricky ground there, because my statement was based on an oral tradition among the villagers.

When I had finished speaking the villagers all applauded, only to be shushed by the chief judge. Their lordships then left the court to make their decision.

When they returned they looked as inscrutable as ever. My heart was in my mouth. They sat down. Then the chief judge said in a slightly pompous voice, "My colleagues and I have decided that natural justice is on the side of the villagers but that the law is on the side of the Baron. However, we have agreed that the law should be based ultimately on natural justice and therefore we have decided in favour of the villagers. The Baron must take down the fence. He must unblock the stream. He must stop the helicopters flying over the village. However, the villagers must pay the Baron one dollar to renew the fishing rights."

There was a great cheer from the villagers. The Baron murdered me with a look.

When the Baron's son got married he went to live on an adjacent estate. The Baron let it be known that it was a much more beautiful estate than his own. That may or may not have been the truth from his point of view, but to the villagers, their village was the most beautiful place in the world. They did have a point, but I couldn't quite agree, because my native village in England is the most beautiful place in the world.

33

The examination cheats

I suppose Lancelot Gammidge was a fairly ordinary sort of person in many ways. But then, many people are ninety nine percent ordinary, and yet have some quirk of genius or some streak of evil which makes them extraordinary. Often enough this one percent of a person never reveals itself. For example, I suspect that I am really a football genius, but I have never had the opportunity to show it. On the other hand, in certain circumstances I might prove to be capable of murder, but the good Lord has so far prevented me from straying in that direction, despite occasional temptations.

Some ten years before I met Lancelot, he and four other university undergraduates had made a solemn pact. They had been involved in an examination fraud and they had sworn on the good book never to reveal this fraud to a living soul. Now that may seem to be an odd cocktail of evil and good, but then in my experience that is what people are, a mixture of evil and good.

Four of the men had passed the examination with flying colours, but one had failed, despite a foreknowledge of the content of the paper. I expect you will have guessed that the one who failed was Lancelot. When he told me the story he said that during the examination the word "cheat" kept beating like a drum in his brain and he couldn't write a single word. I suppose ultimately that may be to his credit. In fact, he sat the examinations again and passed without the need to cheat. The result was that he was the only one of the five with a genuine B.A. The other four held fraudulently obtained B.A.s.

All five men undertook reasonably successful careers. One became a civil servant. The second became a solicitor, after taking further examinations. The third went into his father's factory as a business executive. The fourth became a college lecturer. And Lancelot became a well known figure in the stock market. All five married and they all lived reasonably close to each other and had an annual reunion dinner, the wives not being privy to the sort of reunion it really was. It was called the Rogues' Gathering by the five men. The ladies assumed this was some reference to past amorous activities and found it amusing to speculate as to what these might have been.

One night, when Lancelot and his wife had been particularly amorous he told her during the following pillow talk what the terrible secret of the five men was, swearing her to secrecy. However, she thought that did not include the other wives and told each of them one by one. Thus it was that all five wives knew of the past fraud, but they never talked about it in front of the men. They guessed, probably rightly, that such open conversation on the topic would play havoc with their marital relationships.

All went well until one of the couples obtained a divorce. As you may know, divorce is a messy business. It usually means that one of the partners at least has broken the wedding vows. The acrimony which follows is often lethal and not infrequently it is exacerbated by the convolutions of the court proceedings. In this case, the divorced lady broadcast to all and sundry the story of the examination fraud. Of course, it was clear to everyone that Lancelot was the only one to hold a genuine degree. When the other four discovered that it was Lancelot who had spilled the beans they were bent on revenge. That was when Lancelot came to see me.

When Lancelot had told me his story I said, "Is the university going to withdraw the degrees of the five of you?"

154

"There's no actual evidence of fraud," said Lancelot. "After all, it's some years ago. The only thing is none of us dares ever to go back to the university and the other four are the laughing stock of an area within a radius of fifty miles from the centre of London. Their careers might well be affected, I suppose."

"What have they threatened to do?" I asked.

"I've had telephone calls and several anonymous letters, obviously from them. The general idea is that they will get even, though it's all rather vague. I'm worried sick. I can't sleep. I wish my silly wife had kept her mouth shut."

"But it was you that told her," I couldn't resist saying, "and you had sworn to keep silent."

"I know," he said, groaning. "I regret getting involved in the first place. It's ruining my life. What are my children going to say when they're old enough to understand?"

"That's not the main difficulty, surely. You just have to tell your children both sides of the story and that you got your degree by fair means, whereas you couldn't get it by cheating. That's very moral, in a way. What's worrying me is what mischief these four men are going to get up to. Will it come to violence, do you think?"

He went white at the thought. "It wouldn't surprise me if it did," he said.

We sat quietly for a while. Then I said. "You must go and see a solicitor."

"That would be very embarrassing," he said.

"If a little embarrassment keeps you and your family safe, surely it's worth it."

"What did you have in mind, Brother Tristram?"

"Simply this. Tell the solicitor the whole story, including the threats you have received. Then write to your friends and tell them what you have done. Whatever you do don't threaten them. The knowledge that you have informed a represenatative of the law will frighten them off. There's nothing like the threat of being found out to stop somebody from taking a precipitate and illegal action."

"Are you sure it will work?" he asked nervously.

I paused just ever so slightly. Within that split second I knew that what the man needed above all was reassurance, so even though I wasn't at all sure, I said, "Of course it will work."

That was the last I saw of Lancelot. As I heard no bad news I assumed that this was good news. However, I guessed that he would be looking over his shoulder for a long time to come.

When I thought about this episode I concluded that several people had broken promises and that this had made up a chain of circumstance which had led to the unhappy situation I have described. Perhaps the event which was even more reprehensible than the cheating in the examination was the oath taken on the Bible afterwards. The examiners may be cheated, but God is never cheated. His name cannot be taken in vain lightly. As it says in the good book, "My word does not return to me empty." Neither does a man's word return to him empty. A lie or a broken promise or a promise associated with evil will some day bite back very painfully.

34

Sister Ursula's unfailing nostrum

Two married couples I once knew decided to indulge in a bit of light hearted wife swapping, or husband swapping, if you prefer to put it that way.

John and Mary Wisden had been happily married for twenty years but had become ever so slightly bored with each other. John was a headmaster. Mary had returned to teaching after bringing up the children. William and Judy Walters had also been married for about the same period but had never been happy in their love making. William was an accountant and his wife was an office manager. They had no children. The two couples met at a party in somebody else's house and started to go around in a foursome.

The four became good friends. It was apparent to all of them that they were each attracted to the other's partner. Being of modern outlook, this did not shock them. Indeed, they all four talked about it over dinner one evening.

John said, "I really fancy Judy, you know, William. And I know you fancy Mary. Still, I expect we're all too sensible to do anything about it. Staid middle aged couples, that's what we are."

Mary said, "I know Judy fancies you, John, and certainly I fancy William. What would be the harm in having a little experiment?"

"So long as it's not too kinky," giggled Judy. "What did you have in mind?"

William said, "Why don't John and I accidentally take home the wrong wives, just for one evening. That couldn't possibly do any harm, could it?"

Mary said, "That should be interesting. There's only one snag. What are our children going to think when they find Judy in bed with John the following morning?"

"That's no problem," said John. "We'll send them to granny for the night. They'll think it's a great adventure."

And so it came about that they swapped wives for the one night. I think it's called a one night stand or something. The phrase seems appropriate, at any rate, even if it is not quite accurate. The strange thing is that none of the four actually enjoyed the experience very much. As William said afterwards, "Perhaps we were all too tense."

"The cure for that is simple," said Mary. "Why don't we do it more often. Then we would be more relaxed about it."

"What a splendid idea!" said William, who had really been disappointed with his own performance on the night in question. He felt he had lost face with Mary. He added. "Why don't we do it every Saturday night for a while, just to see how it works out. We're too mature to get worked up about it, aren't we?"

They all readily agreed that this was the case, so they went ahead. Every Saturday night for some months they swapped partners until it became almost habitual. Or so it seemed on the surface. In actual fact, each of the four became very uneasy. This feeling of uneasiness became worse as time went on, but nobody dared say anything. After another two months they all began to snap at each other. Whereas previously they had always had pleasant and amusing conversations, now they found their evenings together painfully embarrassing.

One Wednesday evening John and Mary had a blazing row. It started over the washing up, but they both knew it was really about the wife swapping. Mary said, "You love her more than you love me, don't you?"

John shouted, "She's exciting, that's all."

"Meaning I'm boring!"

"Well, what's William like? Is he a real he man? Does he give you satisfaction?"

Then they started to throw things. However, they managed to patch things up, for a while anyway.

The strange thing is that the following week William and Judy had a blazing row also. Judy accused William of being insanely jealous. He shouted back, "You must be joking. Why should I be jealous because you go to bed with a wimp like John Wisden?"

William gave his wife a black eye and she scratched his face so that he had to stay away from work for several days. However, they too managed to patch things up.

As time went on the rows became more frequent. The wife swapping experiment stopped abruptly and the two couples stopped meeting. However, the rows in each household festered on.

One day William met Mary in the street and they had coffee together. They then started to meet secretly and eventually decided they were in love. Two sets of divorce proceedings followed. Then William and Mary married, taking Mary's children along with them. Surprisingly, John and Judy did not marry. In fact, it was clear they hated the sight of each other. After six months William and Mary found that life was not a bed of roses and decided to part.

So it happened that two happy couples had become four unhappy singles.

William, who was a lapsed member of our church, came to see me one day to ask my advice. I must say I found it very difficult to suggest anything constructive except that he might try to get back together with his first wife. However, William felt that this would be very difficult. I asked him to come back a week later. In the meantime I prayed and also had a chat with Sister Ursula. I told her the story, but did not give her the names of the people concerned. What I was really after was her opinion as to the best course of action.

When I had finished my tale she said, "Brother, it's of no use you prating about the seventh* commandment and the terrible effects of breaking it. You are forgetting the very first principle of counselling. You have to start from where you are. What's needed now is a lot of love and forgiveness."

"How do I persuade them to do that?"

"Very rightly you have withheld the names of these people from me. However, I suggest you tell the man who came to see you to ask his wife if she is at least willing to discuss matters through a third party."

"Who would that be?" I said, hoping she would volunteer.

"You know perfectly well," she said. "It's you I mean. It's no good me talking to her. It's much better coming from a man. You do have the very minimum of charm required."

As you will have noticed Sister Ursula doesn't throw around compliments very freely.

However, I have played chess sometimes, so I was cunning enough to reply, "I will talk to the woman if you'll talk to the man."

"Very well. We'll do what we can."

The upshot was that we managed to bring William and Judy together again. On Sister Ursula's advice they tried successfully to produce a child. However, that still left another one happy couple separated. Unfortunately there was no way I could help them. I could only pray that one of them would go somewhere for help and that it would be forthcoming.

By the way, I must say to you that I never cease to be impressed by the practical streak in Sister Ursula; and beneath that rather forbidding exterior there also beats a heart of gold.

* In some traditions the sixth commandment.

35

How one knot helped to
untie another knot

Last week I met two people who were in great need of help. One was an elderly lady who had just lost her husband. What do you say to somebody who has been married happily for more than fifty years and who is then wrenched away from all that love as suddenly as lightning strikes? I know that priests are supposed to know the answers to questions like that and I suppose we do have stock answers. Unfortunately, the stock answers are not always the right answers in particular situations.

Fairly obviously I said to Mrs Denbigh that her husband was now in heaven and that one day they would be reunited. The trouble with that stock answer is we don't know an awful lot about heaven and the thought of meeting again some time in the future doesn't heal the gaping wound that needs immediate attention. I also said to her, of course, that if she prayed for help God would come himself and help her. Certainly I believe that to be true, but in Mrs Denbigh's case this stock answer didn't seem to work. To build up her confidence I even asked her to repeat one of the Beatitudes several times during the day. I'm sure you know the one I mean. It goes: "Blessed are those who mourn for they shall be comforted."

I was not having a lot of success with Mrs Denbigh so, as I often do when I'm in difficulty, I called on Sister Ursula and was treated to a cup of tea and a huge piece of Victoria sponge cake. When I told Sister Ursula the nature of my problem she said crisply, "The woman wants somebody or something to love. Love is a two way business, you know. She is missing the love of her husband, that's for sure. But what she's missing even more is giving her love. If you've given love to somebody for that long and then it's taken away, it's not surprising she's not finding comfort."

"What did you have in mind, Sister?" I said hopefully. I was hopeful because Mrs Denbigh had now become a central part of my life and I couldn't just walk away. If there was a workable solution to the problem then possibly I would be able to let her go.

Sister Ursula said, "Has the woman not got any grand-children?"

"Unfortunately," I said, "she and her husband produced no offspring. How about a puppy or a kitten?"

"Not good enough, Brother. She needs another human being to love. What a pity families don't adopt elderly people who have no descendants. However, I think I can help. I know a man who is widowed. He has three young children and he often needs somebody to look after them in the evenings. He's in the parish so they can't live too far apart. If she could be in regular contact with three children I would wager that there would be an immediate improve-ment in her condition."

Sister Ursula's advice sounded sensible enough so we agreed to have a word with the two parties concerned. When the system was put into operation I was amazed at the difference in Mrs Denbigh. Obviously, she still missed her husband terribly, but it seemed as if half of the pain had been taken away. When I pondered this miracle I realised that the Beatitude about being comforted had come true. I concluded that the Lord doesn't intervene personally if he has somebody else near at hand to do the job on his behalf.

The second person who came to me for advice was George Biddulph, one of our more well to do church mem-bers. He was a successful solicitor who made most of his money by dealing with divorces. The Church does not, of course, approve of divorces. However, we have to live in the real world and if a person is a solicitor he cannot turn round to his partners and say, "Sorry, divorces are against my principles."

However, it wasn't about his job that George came to see me. It was about his wife, Victoria. On the surface they had a happy marriage and had produced three attractive children. But for whatever reason the couple had become extremely unhappy and Victoria was threatening to leave and planned to take the children with her. George and I chatted around the subject for a while. I was looking for some kind of clue that might enable me to give helpful advice. At one point he said, "You know, Brother Tristram, the tension builds up inside a man and he feels like hitting out."

This remark dropped like the proverbial penny into my consciousness. I said, "Have you actually struck your wife?"

"Not very hard," he said, turning red. "It's more of a slap really."

I asked the next inexorable question, "Have you struck the children?"

He turned even redder and said lamely, "They do need correcting now and again."

Finally I got the full story out of him. He and his wife had been going through a bad patch. Things at work had been very difficult because one of the partners had left, taking a number of clients with him. The frustration had built up over the months and he had been unable to stop himself from violent behaviour at home. I said, "You're lucky you haven't had the social services round."

"They did call," he said. "One of the neighbours complained. But we convinced them there was nothing in it."

"So your wife was very loyal?"

"Yes, of course. But things have gone from bad to worse. I'm worried about what might happen next."

"You've taken the first step," I said. Then it was that the

inspiration came to me. The problem of Mrs Denbigh had suddenly illuminated a completely different sort of problem. I continued, "I think there are three necessary steps to solving this problem. The first, as I have said, you have taken. You are sorry for what you have done. The second step must be to take expert advice from a counsellor in the right field. I can only give you spiritual advice."

"I don't wish to wash my dirty linen in front of an audience," he said sharply.

I realised that he exempted priests from this ban. I understood his reasons for being reluctant to talk to others, so I said, "Bona fide counsellors are bound to confidentiality just as priests are."

"Well…'

"The third step," I said firmly, "is to concentrate on loving your wife and children. You must show them very openly and in very practical ways that you really do love them."

"You know I do!" he said, slightly angry.

"Of course," I said, "but the outward signs are important to people. If you behave as if you don't love them, then they will accept the evidence they experience."

"I think I see," he said. "But how can I stop myself from becoming violent."

"Are you really sorry you have been violent, with every ounce of your being, just as if you were mourning for somebody."

"I don't see what you mean," he said.

"You've lost you're true self. You need to understand the loss and to go into mourning." As he still looked slightly puzzled I added, "It's a roundabout way of making sure you are truly repentant."

That seemed to reach him. So I said with what I hoped was an air of great wisdom, "You know what the Beatitude says. 'Blessed are those who mourn, for they shall be comforted.' You see, if you truly mourn your true self God

164

will comfort you. It also helps if you count to ten. Better still, count to twenty. That's simply a well tried device for giving you time to think before you hit out."

This advice seemed to work. At any rate, George didn't come back to see me and he and his family certainly stayed together.

I find it remarkable how often the Holy Spirit seems to put the right solution before me just in time to solve the next problem.

36

Mrs Wilkinson's Ming vase

Mrs Wilkinson was inconsolable when her Ming vase was stolen. It was the only thing of value she had ever owned and, by all accounts, it was certainly a thing of beauty. Not only was this vase of great monetary value, it was also of enormous sentimental value. That is one of the hardest aspects of being burgled. Not only have strange and careless hands rummaged through all your cupboards, but invariably some of the things stolen are irreplaceable because of past associations.

I called on Mrs Wilkinson the day after the burglary to see if I could help her in any way. She had so often helped other people that she deserved at least a shoulder to cry on. She offered me a cup of tea and a biscuit, which I accepted. While the kettle was boiling she said in a very distressed voice, "You know, Brother Tristram, I am upset, very upset."

Her kindly face was crumpled with unhappiness. A tear glinted behind her glasses.

"It's not so much the value of the vase. And if somebody's hard up they're welcome to my television, my radio and my jewellery. But the Ming vase was so special. It was my late husband's really."

"How did he come by it?" I said, feeling that it would be very good for her to share her memories.

"It was given to him by the Princess of Nawali for services rendered. I know that sounds naughty, but actually it wasn't. Les escorted her and her three daughters through a war services zone and got them home safely to the Palace. He was the sergeant in charge of the section that escorted her. She was so grateful and wanted to give him money, but he refused. However, she insisted he should have something and told him to choose from a selection of five things. Les could remember every detail. He described it to me and I can imagine it, just as if I was there. He could have chosen a jewelled fan. If I'd been married to him then, he said he would have chosen that."

"He must have loved you very much," I said.

"We loved each other," she said, her face dreamy. "Anyway, there were other things to choose from. There was a Chinese clock, but Les didn't think he could get it home in one piece. Then there was an ivory pendant. We saw one like it years later in a catalogue for an auction. Les swore it was exactly the same. It was sold for a fortune and Les wondered if he had chosen the wrong thing. Then he said, 'Well, what's money? It's the thought that counts.'"

"What was the other thing Les could have chosen?" I said.

"It was a miniature portrait of the Princess's father, the Rajah. Les could see she didn't really want to part with it, but that's a measure of her generosity, isn't it? She was prepared to give it to Les because she was so grateful."

"So he chose the vase," I said. "I wonder why he chose it. Did he say?"

"Simply because he liked it. And he wanted to give it to his mother. And he did. When she died it came back to us. So you can see, that's another reason why it means so much to me."

"Yes," I said. "I do see."

The police promised to do their best to trace the vase and there was little I could do to help, except to visit the old lady now and again. The thought uppermost in my mind was how thoughtless people are. I suppose burglars steal to make money, but I wonder if they realise that they are often trampling over people's feelings? It's a bit like scratching all over a picture of a beautiful sunset.

Sometimes providence takes a special hand in sorting out people's problems. At any rate, I believe that some guardian angel was watching over this situation. Twelve months went by and there was no news from the police about where the vase might be. It looked like a lost cause. One of the detectives had said pessimistically to Mrs Wilkinson that if the burglar kept the vase in his own house, then it would be practically impossible to trace it. Stolen valuables are usually traced when they are sold. Perhaps the burglar didn't know the value of the vase.

One day I happened to arrive at Mrs Wilkinson's house at the same time as a smartly dressed young man. At first I thought he was a salesman because he was carrying a case. He wore a smart navy blue suit and his black hair was slicked back neatly. We were both standing on the doorstep when Mrs Wilkinson opened the door. She said, "Oh, do come in Brother Tristram. Who's your friend?"

I quickly explained that I didn't know the other visitor. Then the young man said, "I'm a policeman, Mrs Wilkinson. I want to talk to you about your burglary."

I said, "I'll come back some other time."

But Mrs Wilkinson said, "Don't be silly. You know all about the burglary. Anyway, you can advise me."

The upshot was that a couple of minutes later we were sitting in Mrs Wilkinson's living room. "I'll put the kettle on," she said.

While we were sipping our tea the detective said, "I think we might have found at least one of your stolen items," Mrs Wilkinson.

She looked at him hopefully. I knew what she was hoping.

He continued, "There was a valuable vase, wasn't there?"

"Yes," she said. I could see she was all tensed up.

The detective opened his case. He took out an object wrapped in layers and layers of paper. Carefully he un-wrapped the vase and held it up. "Is this it?" he said.

Mrs Wilkinson cried out in her excitement. "Yes," she said. "That's our Les's vase, all right."

"Can you be certain?" said the detective.

"It has a mark on the bottom," she said. "It's a crown with an elephant underneath."

The detective turned over the vase and said, "That's right Mrs Wilkinson. It's your vase. No doubt about it. But you'll never believe how we came to get it back."

Mrs Wilkinson and I waited expectantly for him to explain. He continued, "This man reported a burglary about a month ago. He gave an exact description of everything that was stolen, including this vase. I've never seen anybody so furious. He was swearing and shouting and going on about people, trampling all over his house and taking his most valuable possessions. Then he went on about the police not doing their job properly. Goodness me, he was demented."

"I was upset myself," said Mrs Wilkinson.

"And understandably so," said the detective. "Anyway the vase turned up in an auction about a week ago, but before it was sold one of our men identified it as a stolen item from your robbery, so the vase was withdrawn. When we took it back to the man who was burgled he swore it was his vase. And then we had him. He was the one who burgled your house, you see."

Mrs Wilkinson and I were open mouthed at this revelation.

The detective said, "Funny, isn't it. When a burglar gets burgled he then begins to understand what hurt can be caused by stealing other people's property. Apparently one of the stolen items was a wedding present and we haven't been able to trace it. His wife is ever so upset."

"What will happen to him?" said Mrs Wilkinson.

"He's already in the nick," said the detective, "Your identification of the vase is just one link in the case against him. I expect he'll go down for several years at least. Apparently he has a lot of other burglaries to account for."

37

The king who changed overnight

When I was a young monk I spent a year or two in a country called Mardala. In the language of that country the name means The Land of the Sacred Dragonfly. The Mardalians thought the dragonfly was sacred because it is so beautiful. Above all the people of that country value beautiful things. The King of Mardala was no exception. When he wanted to marry he got his chief minister to organise a beauty contest in the western style with all the trimmings. Not only had these aspiring beauties to dress in swim suits and ball gowns, they also had to carry on an intelligent conversation. The King had no intention of marrying a dumb blonde, or even a dumb brunette. After much viewing and discussion a suitable girl was found and so King Patu married Mariga and she made a very beautiful Queen. It turned out, in more ways than one, that the King had met his match.

Before his marriage King Patu had been something of a bully. It was more a case of shouting at people than doing them physical harm, though that was because he did not care to touch the common people. Other people did that for him. He was renowned for throwing things, though. Once when a swan pie was slightly off he had thrown it at the unfortunate cook.

Unhappily, he began his married life in his usual bullying way. Queen Mariga was very upset. She didn't like being shouted at and she wasn't used to being ordered about all the time. However, she was a very meek sort of girl and at first accepted the treatment she received from her husband without complaint.

When the two had been married for some months I was called to the palace to give some English lessons to the Queen in order to prepare her for a visit to the United States of America. I was also supposed to give her some background knowledge about America and its culture. Before I started these sessions with her the King interviewed me. It was not a pleasant interview, I can tell you. He asked me all kinds of questions and shouted at me at least seven times, even though I had done nothing wrong. However, I was under the orders of my monastery and I had been warned not to upset the King under any circumstances. Personally, I didn't think it took much to upset him, but like the Queen I behaved in a meek and mild manner. Before the King let me go he warned me that if I made a pass at his wife he would have my skin for a book cover. He wasn't joking. I had seen several books in the library bound with the skins of subjects who had misbehaved. I patiently reassured him that I had taken a vow of celibacy. His final word on the matter was, "I don't care if you've taken twenty vows of celibacy, if you lay a finger on my Queen you will die before the sun rises again."

You may be sure that I avoided touching the Queen as if she had bubonic plague. But I have to admit that I did fell a victim to her charms; at least, as much as a monk is allowed to do. During my sessions with her I had to read various passages from English and American literature. She certainly enjoyed Walt Whitman and Shakespeare, but to my surprise, the book she liked to hear me read most of all was the Christian Bible.

One day she said, "Read me that bit about the blessings of God, Brother Tristram. It is so beautiful. I could listen to it again and again."

That was about the twentieth time I had read it to her and I couldn't help wondering what the attraction was. However, I opened the Bible and began to read;

171

Blessed are the poor in spirit,
fr theirs is the kingdom of heaven.
Blessed are those who mourn,
for they shall be comforted.
Blessed are the meek,
for they shall inherit the earth...".

When I got to that point the Queen said, "Stop there please. That is the bit I like. 'Blessed are the meek, for they shall inherit the earth.' Tell me Brother Tristram, is my husband the King meek?"

I have been in a lot of sticky situations in my time, but that was one of the stickiest. Whichever way I answered I could end up as a book cover. If I said the King was not meek, it might well be true, but if he got to hear about it my fate would be sealed. On the other hand, if I said he was meek, I could be insulting the King and could still end up as a book cover. However, even though I was young I had acquired a measure of diplomatic skill. I said warily, "Your majesty, I am not wise enough to answer that question. You must ask the King himself. Like all kings he has the reputation for being wise."

Queen Mariga gave a tinkling laugh. "You are no fool, Brother Tristram. But let me tell you what is worrying me. I want my husband to be a great king. In your Bible it says that the greatest rulers are humble and meek, does it not?"

"I know the passage you mean," I said, again diplomatically, because some of the greatest kings in the Bible were not exactly meek. However, I had read to her the other day a passage about a king riding meekly on a donkey, and that must have caught her imaginaton.

The Queen then said, "Tell me, is the King popular?"

I was beginning to think my teaching post with the Queen was more dangerous than I had anticipated. I knew that walls had ears in the palace. After a pause during which my mind was frantically racing, I said, "Only the people can answer that question, your majesty."

She laughed again, her dark curls shaking slightly in the most charming way. "I'm sure you will be pope one day, Brother Tristram. You know the answers to both of my questions as well as I do. But I intend to change my husband. I have decided that he will be meek in future. I want him to be popular and I also want him to be great. I do not wish the historians of the future to say that I was married to an unpopular bully. Now I shall ask you a really difficult question. How shall I set about this task?"

I was struck dumb.

"Dear me," she said, "can't you answer a simple question like that, Brother Tristram? Perhaps you will not be pope after all. Thank you, that is all for today."

Do you know, the following day the King was a changed man. He was as meek and mild as a lamb. Whatever had happened during the night I couldn't guess, but the fact is that the King's character was completely changed. I thought at first it was a pure coincidence, but the following day it was the same. And so it went on for a week. Everybody was very nervous because they expected to be shouted at, and when it didn't happen they suspected that the King had something worse up his sleeve. So it went on until it was time for the Queen to go to the United States and for me to go to other duties.

I did have a last interview with the Queen. She thanked me for all my help and gave me a generous cheque for the monastery's school. Before I left the room the Queen said, "Aren't you curious, Brother Tristram?"

I stammered, "What about your majesty?"

"You know perfectly well what about. Tell me, is the King meek and will he be more popular?"

I nodded my assent, not daring to speak on the subject.

"Do you want to know what I did?" she said.

Unfortunately, at that very moment the King himself walked into the room. He said pleasantly, "Ah, my dear friend, Brother Tristram. Let me shake your hand. You have done an excellent job. I trust the Queen has suitably rewarded you."

"Yes, your majesty," I said. "And I have enjoyed my stay here very much."

"You must come again some time. Goodbye."

That was obviously my cue to go. As I left I heard the King say, "My dearest Queen, remember what you told me about a month or so ago...".

As I am more curious than the average cat, it has always been very painful for me to remember that if the King had entered that room five minutes later I might have learnt the Queen's secret. Whatever it was, I wish she would try it on the Prior of my monastery. He's being very bossy at the moment.

Many years later I saw a picture of King Patu in the Times. The Queen was standing beside him and her beautiful smile was the same as ever. The article beneath the picture explained that the King of Mardala had been elected chairman of a great conference of the world's nations. That certainly gave me something to think about, I can tell you.

38

How a bald head started a war

I was in Arcatia at the time. The Prime Minister was a very popular man, except with the Parliamentary opposition who all thought he was a lunatic, and frequently said so. As you will have gathered, free speech was a strong character- istic of Arcatia, but apparently, even in that easy going country there is a limit.

The argument started about the Prime Minister's wife. She was a very handsome woman aged about forty five and was much admired. Her picture often appeared in the fash- ion pages and she was truly a trend setter. If Mrs Drucey started to wear short red dresses, then all the women fol- lowed suit. If she wore a yellow pill box hat, then all the other Arcatian ladies followed. Sometimes, even the Paris fashions were influenced by Mrs Drucey. Her husband, the Prime Minister, lapped all this up. It was good publicity and did him a lot of political good. However, there are two sides to every coin, as the Prime Minister discovered.

One evening Mr and Mrs Drucey were having dinner in a posh hotel accompanied by six foreign potentates. I can tell you that the menu was a sumptuous one. The first course was crane's eggs stuffed with caviare. The second course was salmon and marmalade puree on Abernethy biscuits which had been sent all the way from Scotland for the occasion. The third course was reindeer ankles filled with pomegranate sauce. The fourth course was roast el- ephant's leg with a dressing of pumpkin and coriander. Need I go on? Suffice to say there were fourteen courses altogether.

It was when they reached the Irish coffee stage that the accident happened. I suppose the wine must bear the blame to some extent, because everyone in the party was in high spirits. And then, with several cups each of Irish coffee, they were really over the top. Mrs Drucey offered to do her party piece. This was quite spectacular because at one time she had been a professional acrobat. The tables were cleared and the good lady hitched up her skirts and began to do handsprings and somersaults to the rhythm of a fast South American samba.

What Mrs Drucey had temporarily forgotten under the influence of the wine and the Irish coffee was that she was wearing a wig. It was a gorgeous blonde wig, very similar to her own normally glorious hair. Unfortunately, the Prime Minister's wife had temporary alopecia and all her hair had dropped out. This had been caused by an accident with a new shampoo at her hairdresser's, but it was expected that her own hair would grow back within a year.

To cut a long story short, when this energetic lady was doing a double somersault over a table, her wig fell off and her completely bald head was revealed. There was a gasp of astonishment all round the restaurant. Mrs Drucey quickly put the wig on again and waved gaily at the people on the next table. The Prime Minister explained the cause of the trouble to his guests and everyone heaved a sigh of relief.

Unfortunately the leader of the opposition party got to hear of this event and decided to make some capital out it in Parliament. He made a speech, which was downright insulting, about a Prime Minister who had no taste because he had married a bald headed woman. Then he said in an aside to his own side, "I wonder if she takes it off in bed." This was actually heard all over the house, as was the intention. The Prime Minister immediately stood up and made some insulting remarks about the wife of the leader of the opposition, implying that she was certainly not as handsome as the Prime Minister's wife and that she dyed her hair anyway, so it certainly wasn't her own. Both of these statements were actually true, as most people agreed.

Now if the matter had been left there the whole issue would have gradually fizzled out, but such is human nature that the leader of the opposition continued to pile insults onto the Prime Minister and, of course, the Prime Minister retaliated. One day they came to blows in Parliament. Other people joined in and there was a general scuffle in which several people received bloody noses and broken limbs.

The following day the Prime Minister banned the opposition party. In retaliation the leader of the opposition declared himself Prime Minister. The country was almost equally divided, as were the armed forces. Fighting broke out in the streets between the supporters of the two political parties. Rifle shooting turned into machine gun shooting. Machine gun shooting turned into artillery shooting. Artillery shooting turned into tank fighting. Tank fighting turned into air warfare. In short, a deadly civil war broke out and everybody forgot that it was Mrs Drucey's bald head which had started it all.

The war went on for six months and many people were hurt, but the Arcatians were such terrible shots that very few people were killed by the war, though several died of heart attacks while running away from the bullets. However, there was chaos throughout the land and nobody was happy.

There was only one religion in Arcatia and everybody was supposed to belong to the Arcatian National Church. The name of the national faith was the Many Children of Peace. Naturally the leader of the religion, Patriarch Noah, was very upset by all the fighting, especially when he considered that every Arcatian was supposed to be a Child of Peace. He prayed to God for help and immediately he had an inspiration. He would go to the top of the temple tower at midday on the following day and release some

doves. He would then make a speech through a micro-
phone which was always there on the temple tower for
special occasions. Being a wise man he let this idea slip
accidentally to a member of the press who happened to be
interviewing him about an article he, the Patriarch, had
written in the *Arcatian Times*.

Dawn the following morning gave the promise of a
beautiful day and the sun was shining brightly. Before
noon the Patriarch climbed up the six hundred and twenty
steps to the top of the tower. He was followed by twelve
men each carrying a cage containing a dove. Promptly at
noon the doves were released and then the Patriarch made
his speech, appealing for peace throughout the land. As if
to give a sign, the doves separated into two groups, flew in
opposite directions round the square, and then all joined
together and flew away towards the Parliament building
where they perched and cooed for the rest of the day.

The two opposing leaders watched all this on television
and each decided that enough was enough. Each set off to
walk towards the other's house. They met almost exactly
half way between the two houses. They stopped and looked
at each other. One said, "Were you...?" And the other said,
"Yes, were you...?"

The two men agreed immediately to stop the war. A
week later the Prime Minister announced that the King of
Arcatia had kindly agreed to adopt the dove as a national
symbol. An image of a dove was placed in the centre of the
national flag.

As far as I know there has never been another war in
Arcatia. Mind you, I believe Mrs Drucey gave up acrobat-
ics, even though her hair grew again as luxuriantly as ever
shortly after the war was over.

39

How an embezzler was saved at midnight

There were two brothers, one slightly older than the other. As often happens in families the two were very different. Tom was naturally careful while Tim was always willing to take risks. Tom was a saver, whereas Tim was a spender. Tom was an organiser, but Tim liked to let things happen. Mind you, they had excellent parents who taught them all the good things they should know and warned them against all the bad and dangerous things.

When Tom and Tim grew up their characters were still different, though it is fair to say that Tom had become just a little more adventurous while Tim had become just a little more careful. Perhaps they had influenced each other. Despite their differences they were always good friends and invariably stuck up for each other in arguments, even against their parents.

Strangely, when they married, Tom married a very adventurous girl, while Tim married a very cautious girl. On the face of it that would seem to have been a well balanced arrangement. However, after a few years Tom became more like *his* wife and Tim became more like *his* wife. It was almost as if the two brothers had changed places in the scheme of things. Tom became a spendthrift, while Tim became a saver. Tom began to drink and put bets on horses, whereas Tim never touched a drop and never went into a betting shop.

In due course, the parents of Tom and Tim died, leaving an equal amount of money to each son. It was quite a large amount, enough to retire on if they had wished. However, neither son had it in mind to retire and they continued their work at the respective banks where they were under managers. Neither as yet had achieved a top job as manager, though each of them wished eventually to be the boss in his bank. Still, time was going on and if they didn't get a move on they would miss the boat. At least, that was what their wives told them.

Tom and his wife spent all their inheritance and had to manage on their joint salaries. They had sent their children to an expensive private school. Tom began to bet even more than before and got deeply into debt. For a long time he resisted the temptation to "borrow" from the bank. However, at last he succumbed and for a long time took the bank's money without anyone realising what was going on.

Tim and his wife invested all their inheritance. They both had jobs and saved even more money. They sent their children to the excellent local Comprehensive School, and thus were able to save even more.

So it was that Tom and his wife landed themselves in debt and potentially into very deep trouble. Tim and his wife, however, because of their prudence, became very rich and could afford marvellous holidays, the sort of holiday that Tom could never afford.

I suppose you can only cheat an organisation like a bank for so long before you get caught. Tom's case was no exception. Some bank inspectors came round one day and discovered a large discrepancy in the bank's accounts. However, on the first day of the inspection they hadn't been able to trace exactly what the cause of the discrepancy was. Tom knew that they would certainly find out before the end of the week.

Tom told his wife Gloria what had happened. She started to cry. Tom couldn't stand this weeping so he said, "I'll tell you what. I'll go and talk things over with Tim. Perhaps he can make a sensible suggestion which will get us out of this hole we're in."

So Tom went round to Tim's house. The children were out, but Tim and his wife Kitty were both at home. They were surprised to see Tom and wondered if something was wrong. The brothers did visit fairly frequently, but usually by prearrangement. Tom was offered a cup of coffee and without further ado he confessed to his brother and his sister-in-law what had happened.

"How much money is involved?" asked Tim, when Tom had finished.

"A lot," said Tom, turning very red.

"Tell me, how much?" insisted Tim.

"One hundred and fifty thousand pounds."

Tim whistled. Kitty, his wife, was silent, but looked very shocked.

Tim said, "If you had the money available could you put it back into the bank before the embezzlement is fully discovered?"

Tom went white at the mention of the word "embezzlement". He had always thought of it as borrowing and intended to return the money. He said, "I suppose so. It would take an hour or two to adjust all the accounts though."

"Have you got a key to the bank?" asked Tim.

"I have a master key," said Tom. This was a possession of which he had always been proud.

"Right," said Tim. "We'll go to the bank at midnight and we'll work through the night to put the accounts right. Then in the morning I'll arrange for appropriate transfers from my various personal accounts without my name being involved. With any luck we shall get away with it."

"I didn't know you had that kind of money," said Tom. "Did you win the pools or something?"

"Of course not. Kitty and I have been prudent, that's all."

Kitty was marvellous. She did not complain at all, even though she knew their exotic holidays were at an end and that their savings would be halved.

Both brothers were experts on computers and by five o'clock in the morning the accounts were all square. All that was needed was the payment of the money by Tim into the accounts where money had been missing.

Tom was on pins all morning. He kept going back to the accounts and to the post box. He didn't quite know how Tim was going to pay in the money. At last, by two o'clock in the afternoon, the accounts were put straight, just as the chief inspector was about to do a final check to discover how the discrepancy had arisen.

When the inspector had finished checking he found that the accounts were correct. You should have heard what he said to the assistant inspector who had first discovered there was a discrepancy.

Tom heaved a sigh of relief and settled down to work properly for the first time in a week. Nevertheless he was impatient for five o'clock to come, so that he could rush home to tell Gloria the good news. When he had done that he intended to take Tim and Kitty out for a slap up dinner. However, Tim curtly refused, saying that it was time Tom showed a bit more prudence.

Tom took this to heart. He decided that he had better show a bit more wisdom in future. What he couldn't work out was why Tim had turned out to be the prudent one when he, Tom, who had been prudent as a child, had become a bit of a wally. After a lot of thought he concluded that sometimes people go against their natural bent out of sheer cussedness.

Tim, on the other hand, had cause to ponder the injustices of life. He always remained an under manager while Tom was made the manager of his bank about twelve months after his brother had helped him square the accounts. However, it is fair to say that Tim and Kitty were always the happier couple.

40

The monk who lost his way

To want something is not wrong in itself. It all depends what it is and how much you want it. If you covet another person's husband or wife, then of course that may lead to adultery. If you covet your uncle's fortune, then that may lead to murder, if you want it too much. If you covet an object which you cannot afford to buy, then that may lead to theft. All that seems fairly obvious to everyone.

However, what happens if you covet something good? Suppose you wanted to be a person of good reputation and you bent all your efforts towards being that sort of person. That seems harmless enough. But suppose you took it a stage further and coveted saintliness? The very fact that you wanted it so much might prevent you from getting it, if you see what I mean. Similarly, if you wanted to be the Pope and you let this desire grow out of proportion, then you would become a person completely unsuited for the position. In ancient times people wanted to die for Christ so that they could go straight to heaven and receive a martyr's crown. I'm sure many such people did receive martyrs' crowns and I'm sure they deserved them. At the same time, they didn't normally volunteer to be martyrs. They had martyrdom thrust upon them.

What I'm getting at, apart from the basic idea that coveting can lead you into deep waters, is that to have an ambition to be a saint can also be bad for you. That was Brother Delfont's trouble. He so much wanted to be a good person and he so much wanted to go to heaven that he lost his way altogether. Let me tell you how it all happened.

Brother Delfont and I were at seminary together. He was a great rugby player and scored many a try for the college. Apart from that he wasn't particularly distinguished. I hope you don't think I'm being catty, because I wasn't very distinguished myself and never have been. I'm not the stuff of which bishops are made. That was Brother Delfont's trouble. He so much wanted to distinguish himself as a saint and Christian leader and believed he was the sort of man who could start a revolution in religion. He wanted to be a latter day Saint Francis, or preferably a Saint Ignatius Loyola.

We lived in the same religious house for some years. This was not immediately after seminary. In fact, I had worked in several foreign countries before I came across Brother Delfont again. The day I arrived at that particular monastery I saw Brother Delfont's name on the notice board and I was quite curious to see what time had done to him. Had he developed a slight paunch, as I had? Had he to wear reading glasses as I had? Was he going thin on top, as I was? Was he still undistinguished, as I was?

When I saw him in the dining room later in the day I was astonished to see that he hadn't changed at all. No paunch. No glasses. A full head of hair. And...?

The question in my mind was, what had he done in all the intervening years. Had he, in fact, distinguished himself as a scholar or a missionary? Or had he made a name for himself as a poet or as an artist? We had a chat after dinner, just before we went into chapel. Naturally we shook hands heartily and said things like, "What's old Briggsie doing nowadays?" or "Did you hear what happened to Father John?"

Then the talk became a little more personal. I had to confess that I had done nothing spectacular with my life. Brother Delfont, on the other hand, confessed that he had a great master plan for a revival in the Church. When he told me this his eyes blazed with passion, as if he could see himself leading a great crusade to the New Jerusalem. He said enthusiastically, "I'm sure the Lord is with me. The saints have to be led into the promised land. Would you like to know more details about my new method of meditation?"

Now I'm always a little suspicious about enthusiasm in religion. I'm not too keen on fanaticism either. However, I couldn't very well refuse his invitation.

Incidentally, while we were talking several brothers passed us, one at a time I mean, but each of them had a strange secret smile. I wasn't sure what was amusing them, but I suspected that it was something to do with Brother Delfont's master plan. The following day I went to the chapel with Brother Delfont so that he could show me his method of meditation. I have to say that normally I take meditation very seriously in that context, so if I show scepticism or even amusement at what Brother Delfont told me, then I can assure you I do not normally take that attitude. Mind you, I don't claim to be a great meditator myself, so my view may be rather biassed.

We both sat down and said a prayer. Then Brother Delfont stood and walked to the middle of the chapel where there was a lot of space. He then stood on one foot and inclined his head as in prayer. After five minutes he stood on the other foot and prayed. Then, believe it or not, he did a head stand and stayed in that position for another five minutes. Next, he placed himself horizontally on the floor and did a press up, though he didn't come down. He stayed there with arms stiff and continued to pray. He followed this by taking up other strange positions and praying. The whole prayer session, with all its contortions, lasted for over an hour. Meanwhile I was quietly meditating about other matters. I regret to say that Arsenal's forthcoming game on the following Saturday did enter my mind. Still, I think it is reasonable to pray for the success of a football team, though you may think I'm even more eccentric than Brother Delfont.

When the performance was over – there is no other word I could use – Brother Delfont came over to me and said, "What do you think?"

I must admit I was a bit stumped for words. I said, "Tell me a little more about your method."

"It's simple," he said. "The discipline of the body goes with the discipline of the spirit."

That certainly sounded sensible enough. But then he continued, "It is my intention to train a dedicated group of men and women in my methods and then we shall take over the world. On God's behalf, of course."

I was pleased he added that last little bit, because I was worried in case he was planning to be the Emperor of the Planet, or something equally non – spiritual. However, I gathered he was going to be leader of a great spiritual kingdom stretching from the Americas to Europe and from South Africa to Asia.

To be honest I became quite concerned about Brother Delfont. In fact I went to have a word with the Prior. Now he really was a spiritual man with his mind on higher things. In fact, he was so absent minded that he once opened the front bonnet of his car and thought the engine had been stolen. He had forgotten that the engine was in the boot.

When I explained what was wrong the Prior said, "I know what you're getting at but what can we do? Brother Delfont is quite rational."

"He's flipped his spiritual lid," I said.

"Is that what it's called?" said the Prior, raising his eyebrows slightly.

"Aren't you going to get him to a doctor?" I said.

"Of course not. He'll grow out of it. It's one of the perils of the spiritual life. He's coveting glory instead of humility. God will show him the right way."

He was a wise old bird, the Prior. Within two years Brother Delfont had given up his ambition to be a great spiritual leader and he reverted to something like normal. That, of course, is assuming that there is some kind of normality for monks, or even for anybody in this world.

Index of themes